# VIOLENCE AGAINST WOMEN
## A National and International Perspective

# VIOLENCE AGAINST WOMEN
## A National and International Perspective

**Anuradha Gour**

**MD PUBLICATIONS PVT LTD**
**NEW DELHI**
**www.mdppl.com**

*Published by* :

**MD Publications Pvt Ltd**
"MD House", 11, Darya Ganj,
New Delhi - 110 002
Phone : +91-11-45355555
E-mail : contact@mdppl.com
Website: www.mdppl.com

**ISBN:** 978-81-7533-310-9

Published and Printed by Mr. Pranav Gupta on behalf of **MD Publications Pvt Ltd** at Times Press, Delhi.

# PREFACE

Violence against women is a technical term used to collectively refer to violent acts that are primarily or exclusively committed against women. Similar to a hate crime, this type of violence targets a specific group with the victim's gender as a primary motive. The United Nations General Assembly defines "violence against women" as "any act of gender-based violence that results in, or is likely to result in, physical, sexual or mental harm or suffering to women, including threats of such acts, coercion or arbitrary deprivation of liberty, whether occurring in public or in private life." The 1993 Declaration on the Elimination of Violence against Women noted that this violence could be perpetrated by assailants of gender, family members and even the "State" itself. Worldwide governments and organizations actively work to combat violence against women through a variety of programs. A UN resolution designated November 25th as International Day for the Elimination of Violence against Women.

The United Nations defines violence against women as any act of gender-based violence that results in, or is likely to result in, physical, sexual or mental harm or suffering to women, including threats of such acts, coercion or arbitrary deprivation of liberty, whether occurring in public or in private life.

There are many forms of violence against women, including sexual, physical, or emotional abuse by an intimate partner; physical or sexual abuse by family members or others; sexual harassment and abuse by authority figures (such as teachers, police officers or employers); trafficking for forced labour or sex; and such traditional practices as forced or child marriages, dowry-related violence; and honour killings, when women are murdered in the name of family honour. Systematic sexual abuse in conflict situations is another form of violence against women.

The social and economic costs of violence against women are enormous and have ripple effects throughout society. Women may suffer isolation, inability to work, loss of wages, lack of participation in regular activities, and limited ability to care for themselves and their children.

More evaluation is needed to assess the effectiveness of violence prevention measures. Interventions with promising results include increasing education and opportunities for women and girls, improving their self-esteem and negotiating skills, and reducing gender inequities in communities. Other efforts with positive success include: work with teenagers to reduce dating violence; supportive programmes for children who have witnessed intimate partner violence; mass public education campaigns; and work with men and boys to change attitudes about gender inequities and the acceptability of violence.

I am very grateful to Mr. Pranav Gupta, Director of MD Publications Pvt Ltd, New Delhi, for his kind cooperation and support for this book.

**Anuradha Gour**

# CONTENTS


*Preface* *v*

1. Violence against Women: An Introduction 1
2. Assessing Justice System Response to Violence Against Women 65
3. Specialized Criminal Domestic Violence Courts 83
4. Domestic Violence 109
5. The Enforcing Court: Full Faith and Credit 157
6. Working Effectively with the Police 183

*Bibliography* 207

*Index* 211

# 1

# Violence against Women

## An Introduction

Violence against women is the most pervasive yet least recognized human rights abuse in the world. It also is a profound health problem, sapping women's energy, compromising their physical health, and eroding their self-esteem. Despite its high costs, almost every society in the world has social institutions that legitimize, obscure, and deny abuse. The same acts that would be punished if directed at an employer, a neighbor, or an acquaintance often go unchallenged when men direct them at women, especially within the family.

For over two decades women's advocacy groups around the world have been working to draw more attention to the physical, psychological, and sexual abuse of women and to stress the need for action. They have provided abused women with shelter, lobbied for legal reforms, and challenged the widespread attitudes and beliefs that support violent behavior against women.

Increasingly, these efforts are having results. Today, international institutions are speaking out against gender-based violence. Surveys and studies are collecting more information about the prevalence and nature of abuse. More organizations, service providers, and policy-makers are recognizing that violence against women has serious adverse consequences for women's health and for society.

A growing number of reproductive health programs and practitioners understand that they have a key role to play in addressing violence, not only in helping individual victims but also in preventing abuse. As more becomes known about the scope of gender-based violence and the reasons behind it, more programs are finding ways to address it.

## Meaning of Violence Against Women

The term "violence against women" refers to many types of harmful behavior directed at women and girls because of their sex. In 1993 the United Nations offered the first official definition of such violence when the General Assembly adopted the Declaration on the Elimination of Violence against Women. According to Article 1 of the declaration, violence against women includes:

Any act of gender-based violence that results in, or is likely to result in, physical, sexual or psychological harm or suffering to women, including threats of such acts, coercion or arbitrary deprivations of liberty, whether occurring in public or private life.

There is increasing consensus, as reflected in this declaration, that abuse of women and girls, regardless of where and how it occurs, is best understood within a "gender" framework because it stems in part from women's and girls' subordinate status in society.

Article 2 of the UN Declaration clarifies that the definition of violence against women should encompass, but not be limited to, acts of physical, sexual, and psychological violence in the family and the community. These acts include spousal battering, sexual abuse of female children, dowry-related violence, rape including marital rape, and traditional practices harmful to women, such as female genital mutilation (FGM). They also include non spousal violence, sexual harassment and intimidation at work and in school, trafficking in women, forced prostitution, and violence perpetrated or condoned by the state, such as rape in war.

This issue of *Population Reports* focuses principally on two types of violence: abuse of women within marriage and other intimate relationships and coerced sex, whether it takes place in childhood, adolescence, or adulthood. This focus reflects the types of abuse most dominant in the lives of women and girls around the world.

Other forms of abuse-such as trafficking in women, rape during war, female infanticide, and FGM-are also important. They are not included in this report, however, because they deserve separate consideration. Limiting the focus of the report to intimate partner violence and sexual coercion makes it possible to discuss these issues and appropriate program responses in more depth.

Violence against women is different from interpersonal violence in general. The nature and patterns of violence against men, for example, typically differ from those against women. Men are more likely than women to be victimized by a stranger or casual acquaintance. Women are more likely than men to be victimized by a family member or intimate partner. The fact that women are often emotionally involved with and financially dependent upon those who abuse them has profound implications for how women experience violence and how best to intervene.

## INTIMATE PARTNER ABUSE

Worldwide, one of the most common forms of violence against women is abuse by their husbands or other intimate male partners. Partner violence occurs in all countries and transcends social, economic, religious, and cultural groups. Although women can also be violent and abuse exists in some same-sex relationships, the vast majority of partner abuse is perpetrated by men against their female partners.

While research into intimate partner abuse is in its early stages, there is growing agreement about its nature and the various factors that cause it. Often referred to as "wife- beating," "battering," or "domestic violence," intimate partner abuse is generally part of a pattern of abusive behavior and control rather than an isolated act of physical aggression. Partner abuse can take a variety of forms including physical assault such as hits, slaps, kicks, and beatings; psychological abuse, such as constant belittling, intimidation, and humiliation; and coercive sex. It frequently includes controlling behaviors such as isolating a woman from family and friends, monitoring her movements, and restricting her access to resources.

## MAGNITUDE OF THE PROBLEM

In nearly 50 population-based surveys from around the world, 10% to over 50% of women report being hit or otherwise physically harmed by an intimate male partner at some point in their lives.

Physical violence in intimate relationships almost always is accompanied by psychological abuse and, in one-third to over one-half of cases, by sexual abuse. For example, among 613 abused women in Japan, 57% had suffered all three types of abuse-physical, psychological, and sexual. Only 8% had experienced physical abuse alone. In Monterrey, Mexico, 52% of physically abused women had also been sexually abused by their partners. In León, Nicaragua, among 188 women who were physically abused by their partners, only 5 were not also abused sexually, psychologically, or both.

Most women who suffer any physical aggression generally experience multiple acts over time. In the León study, for example, 60% of women abused in the previous year were abused more than once, and 20% experienced severe violence more than six times. Among women reporting any physical aggression, 70% reported severe abuse. The average number of physical assaults in the previous year among currently abused women surveyed in London was seven; in the US in 1997, three.

In surveys of partner violence, women usually are asked whether or not they have experienced any of a list of specific actions, such as being slapped, pushed, punched, beaten, or threatened with a weapon. Asking behavioral questions-for example, "Has your partner ever physically forced you to have sex against your will?"-yields more accurate responses than asking women whether they have been "abused" or "raped". Surveys generally define physical acts more severe than slapping, pushing, shoving, or throwing objects as "severe violence."

Measuring "acts" of violence does not describe the atmosphere of terror that often permeates abusive relationships. For example, in Canada's 1993 national violence survey one-third of women who had been physically assaulted by a partner said that they had feared for their lives at some point in the relationship. Women often say that the psychological abuse and degradation are even more difficult to bear than the physical abuse.

## DYNAMICS OF ABUSE

Many cultures hold that men have the right to control their wives' behaviour and that woman who challenge that right-even by asking for household money or by expressing the needs of the children-may be punished. In countries as different as Bangladesh, Cambodia, India, Mexico, Nigeria, Pakistan, Papua New Guinea, Tanzania, and Zimbabwe, studies find that violence is frequently viewed as physical chastisement-the husband's right to "correct" an erring wife. As one husband said in a focus-group discussion in Tamil Nadu, India, "If it is a great mistake, then the husband is justified in beating his wife. Why not? A cow will not be obedient without beatings".

Justifications for violence frequently evolve from gender norms-that is, social norms about the proper roles and responsibilities of men and women. Typically, men are given relatively free reign as long as they provide financially for the family. Women are expected to tend the house and mind the children and to show their husbands obedience and respect. If a man perceives that his wife has somehow failed in her role, stepped beyond her bounds, or challenged his rights, then he may react violently.

Worldwide, studies identify a consistent list of events that are said to "trigger" violence. These include: not obeying her husband, talking back, not having food ready on time, failing to care adequately for the children or home, questioning him about money or girlfriends, going somewhere without his permission, refusing him sex, or expressing suspicions of infidelity. All of these constitute transgression of gender norms.

In many developing countries women share the notion that men have the right to discipline their wives by using force Table 1.1. In rural Egypt, for example, at least 80% of women say that beatings are justified under certain circumstances. One of the circumstances that women most often cite is refusing a man sex. Not surprisingly, refusing sex is also one of the reasons women cite most often as triggering beatings.

**Table 1.1. Approval of Wife-Beating**

***Percentage, by Rationale, Selected Studies, 1985–1999***

| *Country & Year (Ref. No.)* | *Respondents* | *She Neglects Children and/or House* | *She Refuses Him Sex* | *He Suspects Her of Adultery* | *She Answers Back or Disobeys* |
|---|---|---|---|---|---|
| *Brazil (Salvodor, Bahia) 1999* | M<br>F | -<br>- | -<br>- | 19[a]<br>11[a] | -<br>- |
| *Chile (Santiago) 1999* | M<br>F | -<br>- | -<br>- | 12[a]<br>14[a] | -<br>- |
| *Colombia (Cali) 1999* | M<br>F | -<br>- | -<br>- | 14[a]<br>13[a] | -<br>- |
| *Egypt 1996* | Urban F<br>Rural F | 40<br>61 | 57<br>81 | -<br>- | 59<br>78 |
| *El Salvodor (San Salvodor) 1999* | M<br>F | -<br>- | -<br>- | 5[a]<br>9[a] | -<br>- |
| *Ghana 1999*[b] | M<br>F | -<br>- | 43<br>33 | -<br>- | -<br>- |
| *India (Uttar Pradesh) 1996* | M | - | - | - | 10–50 |
| *Israel (Palestinians) 1996*[c] | M | - | 28 | 71 | 57 |
| *New Zealand 1995* | M | 1 | 1 | 5[d] | 1[e] |
| *Nicaragua 1999*[f] | Urban F<br>Rural F | 15<br>25 | 5<br>10 | 22<br>32 | -<br>- |
| *Papua New Guinea 1985* | High school F<br>High School M | -<br>- | -<br>- | -<br>- | 59[g]<br>63[g] |
| *Singapore 1996* | M | - | 5 | 33[h] | 4 |
| *Venezuela (Caracas) 1999* | M<br>F | -<br>- | -<br>- | 8[a]<br>8[a] | -<br>- |

*F = Female*

*M = Male*

*Note: - indicates this question not asked*

[a]*An unfaithful woman deserves to be beaten*

[b]*Also, 51% of men and 43% of women agreed: "husband is justified in beating" his wife if she uses family planning without his knowledge.*

[c]*Also, 23% agreed "wife-beating is justified" if she does not respect her husband's relatives.*

[d]*He catches her in bed with another man.*

[e] *She won't do what she is told.*

[f]*Also, 11% of urban women and 23% of rural women agreed "husband is justified in beating" his wife if she goes out without his permission.*

[g]*She speaks disrespectfully to him.*

[h]*She is sexually involved with another man.*

Compiled by the Center for Health and Gender Equity for Population Reports

Societies often distinguish between just and unjust reasons for violence, as well as between acceptable and unacceptable amounts of aggression. The notion of "just cause" permeates findings on violence in many countries. Certain individuals, usually husbands and elders, may have the right to chastise a woman physically for certain transgressions, but only within limits. If a man oversteps these limits by becoming too violent or for beating a woman without "just cause," others have cause to intervene. As a woman in Mexico put it, "If I have done something wrong..., nobody should defend me. But if I haven't done something wrong, I have a right to be defended".

Even where culture itself grants men substantial control over female behavior, abusive men generally exceed the norm. For example, data from the Nicaragua Demographic and Health Survey (DHS) show that, among women who were abused physically, 32% had husbands who scored high on a scale of marital control compared with only 2% among women who were not abused physically. The scale included such behavior as the husband's continually accusing his wife of being unfaithful and limiting her access to family and friends.

## WOMEN'S RESPONSE TO ABUSE

Most abused women are not passive victims but use active strategies to maximize their safety and that of their children. Some women resist, others flee, and still others attempt to keep the peace by capitulating to their husbands' demands. What may seem to an observer to be lack of response to living with violence may in fact be strategic assessment of what it takes for the woman to survive in the marriage and to protect herself and her children.

A woman's response to abuse is often limited by the options available to her. Women consistently cite similar reasons that they remain in abusive relationships: fear of retribution, lack of other means of economic support, concern for the children, emotional dependence, lack of support from family and friends, and an abiding hope that "he will change". In developing countries women cite the unacceptability of being single or unmarried as an additional barrier that keeps them in destructive marriages.

At the same time, denial and fear of social stigma often prevent women from reaching out for help. In surveys, for example, from 22% to almost 70% of abused women say that they have never told anyone about their abuse before being asked in the interview Table 1.2. Those who reach out do so primarily to family members and friends. Few have ever contacted the police.

Despite the obstacles, many women eventually do leave violent partners-even if after many years, once the children are grown. In León, Nicaragua, for example, the likelihood that an abused woman will eventually leave her abuser is 70%. The median time that women spend in a violent relationship is five years. Younger women are more likely to leave sooner.

Studies suggest a consistent set of factors that propel women to leave an abusive relationship: The violence gets more severe and triggers a realization that "he" is not going to change, or the violence begins to take a toll on the children. Women also cite emotional and logistical support from family or friends as pivotal in their decisions to leave.

**Table 1.2. Help-Seeking by Physically Abused Women Selected Studies, 1993-1999**

| *Country & Year (Ref. No.)* | *% of Abused Women Who:* | | | |
|---|---|---|---|---|
| | *Never Told Anyone* | *Contacted Police* | *Told Friends* | *Told Family* |
| *Bangladesh 1993* | 68 | - | - | 30 |
| *Canada 1993* | 22 | 26 | 45 | 44 |
| *Cambodia 1996P* | 34 | 1 | 33 | 22 |
| *Chile 1993* | 30 | 16 | 14 | 32[a] |
| *Egypt 1995–96* | 47 | - | 3 | 44 |
| *Ireland 1995P* | - | 20 | 50 | 37 |
| *Moldova 1997* | - | 6 | 30 | 31 |
| *Nicaragua 1998* | 37 | 17 | 28 | 34 |
| *United Kingdom 1993P* | 38 | 22 | 46 | 31 |

*[a]32% told her family; 21% told his family.*

*"P" after year indicates year of publication for studies not reporting field work dates.*

*Compiled by the Center for Health and Gender Equity for Population Reports.*

Leaving an abusive relationship is a process. The process often includes periods of denial, self-blame, and endurance before women come to recognize the abuse as a pattern and to identify with other women in the same situation. This is the beginning of disengagement and recovery. Most women leave and return several times before they finally leave once and for all.

Regrettably, leaving does not necessarily guarantee a woman's safety. Violence sometimes continues and may even escalate after a woman leaves her partner. In fact, a woman's risk of being murdered is greatest immediately after separation.

## EXPLAINING INTIMATE PARTNER ABUSE

While intimate partner abuse is widespread, it is not universal. Anthropologists have documented small-scale societies-such as the Wape of Papua New Guinea-where domestic violence is virtually absent (95, 275). This finding stands as testament to the fact that social relations can be organized in a way that minimizes partner abuse.

In many places the prevalence of such violence varies substantially among neighboring areas. These local differences are often greater than the differences among countries. For example, in Uttar Pradesh, India, the percentage of men who said they beat their wives varied from 18% in Naintal District to 45% in Banda. The percentage that physically forced their wives to have sex varied from 14% to 36% among districts Table 1.3.

**Table 1.3. Variations in Men's Attitudes and Rates of Abuse Selected Districts, Uttar Pradesh, India, 1995-1996**

| *District* | *% Who Admit to Forcing Wife To Have Sex* | *% Who Agree That If Wife disobeys, She Should Be Beaten* | *% Who Admit to Hitting Wife* | *% Who Hit Wife in Last Year* |
|---|---|---|---|---|
| *Aligarh* | 31 | 15 | 29 | 17 |
| *Banda* | 17 | 50 | 45 | 33 |
| *Gonda* | 36 | 27 | 31 | 20 |
| *Kanpur Nagar* | 14 | 11 | 22 | 10 |
| *Naintal* | 21 | 10 | 18 | 11 |
| *Source: Narayana 1996* | | | | |

Why is violence more widespread in some places than in others? While studies do not provide clear answers, they do identify some characteristics of societies and of relationships that help explain differences in prevalence of violence against women.

## VIOLENCE AND SOCIOECONOMIC STATUS

Although domestic violence occurs in all socioeconomic groups, studies find that women who live in poverty are more likely to experience violence than women of higher status.

It is unclear, however, why poverty increases the risks of violence-whether it is due to low income itself or to other factors that accompany poverty, such as crowding or hopelessness. For some men, living in poverty is likely to generate stress, frustration, and a sense of inadequacy for having failed to live up to their culturally defined role of provider. Poverty may also provide cause for marital disagreements and at the same time make it difficult for women to leave violent or otherwise unsatisfactory relationships.

Low socioeconomic status probably reflects a variety of conditions that in combination increase women's risk of victimization. Increasingly, experts are using an "ecological model" to understand the interplay of personal, situational, and socio cultural factors that combine to cause abuse Figure 1.1. An ecological approach to abuse argues that that no one factor alone "causes" violence but rather that a number of factors combine to raise the likelihood that a particular man in a particular setting may act violently toward a woman.

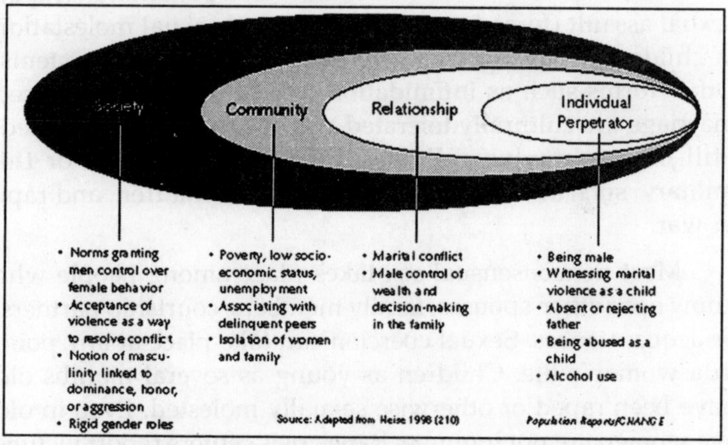


**Figure 1.1. Ecological Model of Factors Associated with Partner Abuse**

In the ecological framework, social and cultural norms-such as those that assert men's inherent superiority over women-combine with individual-level factors-such as whether a man was abused himself as a child-to determine the likelihood of abuse. The more risk factors present, the higher the likelihood of violence.

Other factors of the social environment combine to protect some women. For example, when women have authority and power outside the family, rates of abuse in intimate partnerships appear to be lower. Likewise, prompt intervention by family members appears to reduce the likelihood of domestic violence, as does the presence of all-woman collectives. By contrast, where the family is considered "private" and outside public scrutiny, rates of wife abuse are higher.

## SEXUAL COERCION

Sexual coercion exists along a continuum, from forcible rape to nonphysical forms of pressure that compel girls and women to engage in sex against their will. The touchstone of coercion is that a woman lacks choice and faces severe physical or social consequences if she resists sexual advances.

Some forms of coercion-such as forced penetration (rape), sexual assault (forced sexual contact), and sexual molestation of children-are recognized as crimes by many legal systems. Other forms-such as intimidation, verbal pressure, or forced marriage-are culturally tolerated and at times even condoned. Still others involve collusion by organized crime or the military, such as trafficking in women and children, and rape in war.

Most nonconsensual sex takes place among people who know each other-spouses, family members, courtship partners, or acquaintances. Sexual coercion can take place at any point in a woman's life. Children as young as several months old have been raped or otherwise sexually molested. Even in old age women are not immune: Rape crisis centers report victims in their seventies and older.

Much sexual coercion takes place against children or adolescents in both industrial and developing countries. Between one-third and two-thirds of known sexual assault victims are age 15 or younger, according to information from justice systems and rape crisis centers in Chile, Peru, Malaysia, Mexico, Panama, Papua New Guinea, and the US. During childhood young girls can become easy targets for older male relatives or friends who obtain sex through force or deception. Later, boyfriends, teachers, relatives, or other men in authority may force young women into unwanted sexual encounters.

## FORCED SEX IN MARRIAGE

Ironically, much nonconsensual sex takes place within consensual unions. Not all women experience sex negatively, of course, and many experience pleasure. For some, however, sex is just another medium for male control.

For example, in a 15-country qualitative study of women's HIV risk, women related profoundly troubling experiences of sex within marriage. Respondents frequently mentioned being physically forced to have sex and/or to engage in types of sexual activity that they found degrading and humiliating. Others gave in to sex out of fear of the consequences of refusal, such as physical abuse, loss of economic support, or accusations of infidelity. Many other studies have noted this type of "defensive acquiescence".

In Papua New Guinea, for example, among 95 women interviewed in depth, about half said their husbands had forced them into sex. One-third of those forced said they had been beaten into sex, and one-fifth had been harangued into it by a drunken husband. In Uttar Pradesh, India, about two-thirds of 98 respondents reported being forced into sex by their husbands-about one-third of them by beatings.

## FORCED SEXUAL INITIATION

For a substantial minority of women, sexual initiation is a traumatic occurrence accompanied by force and fear. For others, sexual initiation, although not physically forced, is nonetheless unwanted-an experience they perceive as happening to them rather than as something they choose Table 1.4.

For example, at an antenatal clinic in the outskirts of Cape Town, South Africa, 32% of 191 teenage mothers, whose average age was 16, reported that their first intercourse had been forced. Some 72% reported having had sex against their will at some point, and 11% said they had been raped. Seventy-eight percent said they would be beaten if they refused sex, 39% feared being laughed at, and 6% said they would lose their friends. Some 58% said their sexual partner had beaten them ten or more times. Also, in a study in the Eastern Cape of South Africa, the reasons that young girls most often gave for beginning sex was being "forced by partner," at 28%, followed by "peer pressure," at 20%. Adolescent boys admit that coercion of female partners is common. In Kenya, for example, boys ages 12 to 14 and 15 to 19 in focus-group discussions observed, "We seduce them at first, but if they remain adamant we force them," including sometimes drugging them or gagging them to prevent screams. During focus-group discussions in South Africa, one teenage girl observed, "I actually think forced sex is the norm. It is the way people interact sexually".

**Table 1.4. Prevalence of Forced First Intercourse**

**Selected Studies, 1989-1999**

| *Country & Year (Ref. No.)* | *Sample* | | | *% Whose First Intercourse was Forced* |
|---|---|---|---|---|
| | *Size* | *Type* | *Age* | |
| *Argentina 1998* | 201 | Clinic-based | 15–18 | 6 (41[a]) |
| *Central African Rep. 1989* | 1,307 | National | 15–50 | 21 |
| *Jamaica 1997* | 51[b] | School-based | 8th Grade | 12 |
| *Kenya 1994* | 9,997 | School-based | 12–24 | 8 forced<br>6 "tricked" |
| *Mozambique 1993* | 189 | School-based | 12–23 | 8 |
| *New Zealand 1993–94* | 458 | National, longitudinal | 18 & 21 | 7<br>25[c] |
| *Sierra Leone 1998P* | 144 | Convenience | adult | 31 |
| *South Africa 1999* | 544[b] | Match case-control | <19 | 32 pregnant<br>18 nonpregnant |
| *United States 1992* | 1,663 | National | 18–59 | 4 (25[a]) |

[a]*Unwanted but not forced*

[b]*Sexually active girls only*

[c]*Of those sexually active before age 14*

[d]*Of those sexually active before age 15*

*"P" after year indicates year of publication for studies not reporting field work dates.Compiled by the Center for Health and Gender Equity (CHANGE) for Population Reports.*

The younger a woman is at first sexual intercourse, the more likely that sex is forced. In New Zealand, for example, one girl in every four who had intercourse before age 14 reported that she was forced to do so, often by a much older man. Likewise in the US, 24% of those who had intercourse before age 14 reported having been forced.

Even when first intercourse takes place within marriage, it can be traumatic, especially where women and girls are given little information about sex. A study among married women in a poor community of India reported that many women found their first sexual experience to be traumatic; only 18% had even a vague idea of what to expect on their wedding night. One woman recalled, "It was a terrifying experience. When I tried to resist, he pinned my arms above my head".

Girls who are married off at a young age are especially vulnerable. Although the practice of child marriage is declining, many young girls still are married off unwillingly, often to men many years their elder.

Intercourse at young ages, even when culturally supported, can be traumatic for girls. For example, when anthropologist Mary Hegland interviewed Iranian women living in the US about their sexual initiation in Iran, many recounted graphic stories of forced defloration. Often, relatives held a girl down while the man forced himself on her. The interviewed women used terms like "rape" and "torture" to describe their experience but said that the word "rape" would never be applied to these experiences in Iran because the sex took place within marriage.

## SEXUAL ABUSE IN CHILDHOOD

Sexual abuse of children is widespread in virtually all societies. Child sexual abuse refers to any sexual act that occurs between an adult or immediate family member and a child, and any nonconsensual sexual contact between a child and a peer. Laws generally consider the issue of consent to be irrelevant in cases of sexual contact by an adult with a child, defined variously as someone under 13, 14, 15, or 16 years of age. Because of the taboo nature of the topic, it is difficult to collect reliable statistics on the prevalence of sexual abuse in childhood. The few representative sample surveys that exist report that such abuse is widespread Table 1.5. The studies are not directly comparable because of differences in samples and in definitions of abuse. Most distinguish between abuse that involves physical contact and abuse that does not, such as exhibitionism. They also report on different types of sexual contact-for example, genital touching versus intercourse.

Although both girls and boys can be victims of sexual abuse, most studies report that the prevalence of abuse among girls is at least 1.5 to 3 times that among boys, and sometimes much more. In Barbados, for example, 30% of women and 2% of men reported behavior constituting sexual abuse in childhood or adolescence. Abuse among boys may be underreported compared with abuse among girls, however.

Women tend to report being more profoundly affected by sexual abuse than do men, although some men and boys undoubtedly suffer greatly. The experience of being penetrated appears to be especially traumatic for both boys and girls.

Studies consistently show that, regardless of the sex of the victim, the vast majority of perpetrators are male and are known to the victim. Many perpetrators were themselves sexually abused in childhood, although most boys who are sexually abused do not grow up to abuse others.

Sexual abuse can lead to a wide variety of unhealthy consequences, including behavioral and psychological problems, sexual dysfunction, relationship problems, low self-esteem, depression, thoughts of suicide, alcohol and substance abuse, and sexual risk-taking. Women who are sexually abused in childhood also are at greater risk of being physically or sexually abused as adults.

Although for some children the effects of sexual abuse are severe and long-term, not all will experience consequences that persist into later life. Sexual abuse is most likely to cause long-term harm when it extends over a long period, is by a father or father figure, involves penetration, or involves force or violence.

**Table 1.5. Prevalence of Child Sexual Abuse**

**Selected Studies, 1990-1998**

| *Country & Year (Ref. No.)* | *Study Method & Sample* | *Definition of Child Sexual Abuse* | *Prevalence* |
|---|---|---|---|
| *Antigua 1993* | Probability sample of 97 women. | Sexual contact that is unwanted or with a biological relative; or <16 with perpetrator 5+ years older | 11% of women report sexual exploitation before age 20 |
| *Australia 1997* | Retrospective study of 710 women | Sexual contact <12 with perpetrator 5+ years older; or unwanted sexual activity at ages 12–16 | 20% of women report abuse |
| *Barbados 1993* | National random sample of 264 women | Sexual contact that is unwanted or with a biological relative; or <16 with perpetrator 5+ years older | 30% of women report abuse |
| *Canada 1990* | Population survey of 9,953 men and women age 15+ | Unwanted sexual activity, contact and noncontact, while growing up | 13% of women, 4% of men report abuse |
| *Costa Rica 1992P* | Retrospective survey of university students | Unwanted sexual activity, contact and noncontact; no ages specified | 32% of women, 13% of men report abuse |
| *Germany 1992* | Multiple-screen questionnaire answered by 2,151 students in Würzburg and Leipzig | Distressing sexual activity, contact and noncontact, <14; or with perpetrator 5+ years older | In Würzburg 16% of girls, 6% boys; in Leipzig 10% of girls, 6% of boys report abuse |
| *Malaysia 1996* | Retrospective self-administered questionnaire answered by 616 paramedical students | Vaginal or anal penetration, or unsolicited sexual contact, or witnessing exhibitionism <18 | 8% of women, 2% of men report abuse |
| *New Zealand 1997* | Birth cohort of 520 girls, studied from birth to age 18 | Unwanted sexual activity, contact and noncontact, <16 | 14% of girls report contact abuse; 17% report any abuse |

| *Nicaragua 1997* | Anonymous self-administered questionnaire answered by 134 men and 202 women ages 25–44 drawn from population-based sample | Sexual contact, including attempted penetration, <13 with perpetrator 5+ years older; or nonconsensual activity >12 | 26% of women, 20% of men report abuse |
|---|---|---|---|
| *Norway (Oslo) 1996* | Population-based sample of 465 adolescents, ages 13–19, followed for 6 years | Sexual contact, including "intercourse after pressure," occurring between a child <13 and an adult >17; or involving force | 17% of girls, 1% of boys report abuse |
| *Spain 1995* | Face-to-face interviews and self-administered questionnaires answered by 895 adults ages 18–60 | Unwanted sexual activity, contact and noncontact, <17 | 22% of women and 15% of men report abuse |
| *Switzerland (Geneva) 1996* | Self-administered questionnaire answered by 1,193 ninth grade students | Unwanted sexual activity, contact and noncontact | 20% of girls, 3% of boys report contact abuse; 34% of girls, 11% of |
| *Switzerland (national) 1998* | National survey of 3,993 girls, ages 15–20, enrolled in schools or professional training programs | "Sexual victimization," defined as "when someone in your family, or someone else, touches you in a place you didn't want to be touched, or does something to you sexually which they shouldn't have done." | 19% of girls report abuse |
| *United States 1997* | National 10-year longitudinal study of women's drinking that included questions about | Unwanted sexual activity, contact and noncontact, <18; or <13 with perpetrator 5+ years older | 21% of women report abuse |

*"P" after year indicates year of publication for studies not reporting field work dates.*

*Compiled by the Center for Health and Gender Equity (CHANGE) for Population Reports.*

A child's resilience and the response a child receives when disclosing the abuse also affect the long-term consequences.

When children who disclose abuse are believed and supported, the consequences are often less severe than when disclosure is met with disbelief, blame, or rejection.

## IMPACT ON WOMEN'S REPRODUCTIVE HEALTH

Physical and sexual abuse lie behind some of the most intractable reproductive health issues of our times-unwanted pregnancies, HIV and other sexually transmitted infections, and complications of pregnancy. A growing number of studies document the ways in which violence by intimate partners and sexual coercion undermines women's sexual and reproductive autonomy and jeopardize their health.

Violence operates through multiple pathways to affect women's sexual and reproductive health. Physical violence and sexual abuse can put women at risk of infection and unwanted pregnancies *directly*, if women are forced to have sex, for example, or fear using contraception or condoms because of their partners' reaction. A history of sexual abuse in childhood also can lead to unwanted pregnancies and STIs *indirectly* by increasing sexual risk-taking in adolescence and adulthood.

## SEXUAL AUTONOMY AND UNWANTED PREGNANCIES

In many parts of the world marriage is interpreted as granting men the right to unconditional sexual access to their wives and the power to enforce this access through force if necessary. Women who lack sexual autonomy often are powerless to refuse unwanted sex or to use contraception and thus are at risk of unwanted pregnancies.

As a 40-year old woman in Uttar Pradesh said, "What can I do to protect myself from these unwanted pregnancies unless he agrees to do something? Once when I gathered the courage and told him I wanted to avoid sex with him, he said, 'What else have I married you for?' He beats me for the smallest reasons and has sex whenever he wants".

Not surprisingly, many women acquiesce to having sex even if they do not want it. For example, in the Western Visayas region of the Philippines, 43% of the married women of reproductive age who were surveyed said they were afraid to refuse their husbands' sexual advances, often because refusal might cause their husbands to beat them.

Many studies have found that violence toward women is more common in families with many children. Researchers have long assumed that having many children increases women's risk of being abused, perhaps by increasing levels of stress within the family or provoking more marital disagreements. Recent research in Nicaragua, however, suggests that the relationship may be the reverse, with domestic violence increasing the likelihood that a woman will have many children. The study found that abused women were twice as likely as other women to have four or more children. But 50% of all physical abuse began within the first two years of the relationship, and 80% began within four years. The fact that abuse preceded having many children suggests that violence is a risk factor for having many children, rather than a consequence.

A large-scale survey among married men in Uttar Pradesh, India, demonstrates directly that forced sex can lead to unintended pregnancies. Men who admitted having forced their wives to have sex were 2.6 times more likely than other men to have caused an unplanned pregnancy.

## CONTRACEPTIVE USE

Many women are afraid to raise the issue of contraception for fear that their partners might respond violently. In some cultures husbands may react negatively because they think that protection against pregnancy would encourage their wives to be unfaithful. Where having many children is a sign of virility, a husband may interpret his wife's desire to use family planning as an affront to his masculinity. In Kenya some men say that they oppose the use of contraception because they fear it will weaken their control over their wives.

A woman's perception of her husband's attitude toward family planning strongly influences whether or not she will use contraception, according to studies in Ghana, Indonesia, Kenya, the Philippines, and elsewhere. Across 13 DHS surveys an average of 9% of married women with unmet need for family planning-that is, women who want to avoid pregnancy but are not using any contraceptive method-cite their husbands' disapproval as the principal reason that they do not use contraception. While in surveys only a minority of wives and husbands appear to disagree about using contraception, in-depth studies suggest that these couples probably represent a large share of couples with unmet need.

Women often use contraception clandestinely because they fear being beaten or abandoned if they do so openly. If a woman is caught in covert use of contraception, the consequences of undermining male authority can be severe. In Ghana 51% of women and 43% of men agreed that a husband is justified in beating his wife when she uses a family planning method without his knowledge.

When asked what happens if a woman practices family planning without her husband's consent, men interviewed in Ghana gave such replies as, "It is fitting enough to beat her for not consulting you earlier before going ahead to practice family planning," and "It is not good for you to keep such a woman since she did so without first consulting with you". In Cape Town, South Africa, young women described how their partners beat them and tore up their clinic contraceptive cards.

For women living with men who are violent, the fear of a negative reaction is often enough to cut off discussion of contraception. As one woman said of her husband, "Whenever he hears people discussing family planning over the radio, he fumes and shouts.... If he can threaten a wireless, what would he do to me if I open the topic?"

Fortunately, not all women who fear a negative response are necessarily at risk of abuse. Studies suggest that many husbands are more open to family planning than their wives may think. Communication within marriage about sex is often so limited, however, that spouses often do not know their partners' views of family planning. Wives whose husbands actually favor family planning may assume that their husbands' attitudes mirror cultural norms that disapprove of it. In Uganda, for example, 24% of women thought their husbands disapproved of contraception when in fact their husbands approved.

## VIOLENCE LEADS TO HIGH-RISK SEXUAL BEHAVIOR

Children who have been sexually abused often engage in sexual behavior, as adolescents and as adults, that puts them at risk of unintended pregnancies and sexually transmitted infections. Some researchers view the risky sexual behavior of abuse victims as an effort to gain control or mastery of a childhood experience in which they felt violated and powerless. Others note that the experience of incest and sexual abuse can make it difficult for victims to form healthy intimate relationships. One researcher has observed that a victim's "heightened need for intimacy, coupled with the sexualization of affection, may lead her to seek warmth and closeness through repeated sexual encounters".

## ADOLESCENT PREGNANCIES

Victims of sexual abuse in childhood appear more likely than other teens to become pregnant in adolescence. In the early 1990s studies in the US began to find a consistent association between sexual abuse in childhood and adolescent pregnancy.

The studies also found a clear and consistent link between early sexual victimization and a variety of risk-taking behaviors, including early sexual debut, drug and alcohol use, more sexual partners, and less contraceptive use.

Noting that programs have had difficulty reducing rates of adolescent pregnancy by providing sex education and access to contraception alone, researchers suggested that sexual victimization in childhood might help explain high-risk sexual activity and pregnancies among adolescents. Some have questioned whether it is the sexual victimization itself that contributes to the risk of adolescent pregnancy or whether both are caused by some third factor, such as an unhealthy and disorganized home life. Studies have shown that many of the factors that predispose a young child to sexual abuse, such as absent or dysfunctional parents are also risk factors for adolescent pregnancy.

Although the question is not fully resolved, three recent studies that examined the independent effects of sexual abuse and other factors suggest that sexual abuse itself has an effect on adult sexual behavior beyond the effect of family background. In all three studies victimization in childhood made an independent contribution to problems of mental health, sexuality, and social functioning in adults.

Researchers continue to explore the exact mechanism through which sexual abuse increases the risk of teenage pregnancy. Sexual abuse appears to contribute to teen pregnancy indirectly, by lowering the age at first intercourse and by increasing sexual risk-taking among young people. Studies in Barbados, New Zealand, Nicaragua, and the US confirm that, on average, sexual abuse victims start having voluntary sex significantly earlier than non victims. Such studies also link sexual abuse to a variety of high-risk sexual behaviors in adolescence, including having sex with many partners, using drugs and abusing alcohol, not using contraception, and trading sex for money or drugs.

Childhood abuse has also been linked to unintended pregnancies among adult women. A study of 1,200 women in the US found that women who reported being psychologically, sexually, and/or physically abused, or whose mother was beaten by a partner, had higher rates of unintended first pregnancies than women who did not experience abuse. The likelihood that a woman's first pregnancy was unintended increased with both the number of different types of abuse she experienced and the frequency of abuse.

## STI'S INCLUDING HIV/AIDS

Sexual abuse in childhood appears to increase the risk of sexually transmitted infections (STIs) among adults, largely through its effect on high-risk sexual behavior. Several studies have linked a history of sexual abuse to selling sex for money or drugs. For example, researchers in Rhode Island, US, found that men and women who had been raped or forced to have sex in either childhood or adolescence were four times more likely than people who had not been abused to have worked in prostitution. They were also twice as likely to have multiple sexual partners in a single year and to have casual sex. Among women, victims of childhood sexual assault were twice as likely to be heavy consumers of alcohol and nearly three times as likely to become pregnant before the age of 18. While the abused women studied did not have higher rates of HIV, men who had experienced childhood sexual abuse were twice as likely to be HIV positive as men who did not, independent of a history of intravenous drug use or prostitution.

In a nationally representative study of men and women in Barbados, anthropologist Penn Handworker found that sexual abuse was the most important determinant of high-risk sexual activity during adolescence, including both young age at first sexual intercourse and a high number of sexual partners. The direct effects of childhood sexual abuse on number of partners remained significant into the respondents' mid-thirties. For men, abuse in childhood also was closely linked to not using condoms in adulthood, even after accounting for other variables affecting condom use.

Abuse in childhood also increases the risk of sexually transmitted infection through its effect on drug use. Sexually abused or assaulted women often turn to drugs as a coping mechanism, in addition to engaging in such unhealthy behavior as unprotected sex and trading sex for money or drugs.

In a study at an outpatient methadone maintenance clinic in the South Bronx of New York, early sexual abuse-especially incest-emerged as one of the most formative experiences in the lives of women addicted to such drugs as crack, cocaine, and heroin. A "sense of stigmatization and shame" leaves victims feeling "unloved, unlovable, and unable to say 'no' to things they do not want to do such as having sex or using drugs," researchers concluded.

Not surprisingly, victims of other types of violence, most notably partner abuse, are also at increased risk of STIs. In the US state of North Carolina, for example, women who reported physical and sexual abuse by a partner were more than twice as likely to have experienced STIs as were other women, even after accounting for confounding variables. Data from India suggest that abusive men may be more likely to expose their wives to infection. Abusive men were significantly more likely to have engaged in extramarital sex and to have STI symptoms than were non abusive men.

## VIOLENCE COMPROMISES HIV PROTECTION

In a recent speech Peter Piot, the Executive Director of UNAIDS, noted that violence against women has many links to HIV/AIDS. "Violence against women is not just a cause of the AIDS epidemic," he pointed out. "It can also be a consequence of it".

## CONDOM NEGOTIATION

Violence influences the risk of HIV and other STIs directly when it interferes with women's ability to negotiate condom use. For many women, asking for condoms can be even more difficult than discussing other contraceptives because condoms are often associated with promiscuity, infidelity, and prostitution.

Raising the issue of condom use within marriage or other primary partnerships is especially difficult. As a 46-year-old respondent in Brazil said, "If I ask my husband to use a condom now, he is going to ask 'why?' He is going to think I am fooling around or that I am accusing him of fooling around, two things that shouldn't be happening".

The summary report of the Women and AIDS Research Program of the International Center for Research on Women (ICRW) concludes that "initiating condom use is simply not practical for many women around the globe". In Guatemala, India, Jamaica, and Papua New Guinea, women reported that bringing up condom use-with its implication that one partner or the other has been unfaithful-risks a violent response.

Women in Brazil, Haiti, Rwanda, South Africa, Uganda, and the US have voiced similar fears. In South Africa the notion that violent indignation is an appropriate response to women requesting condoms was so ingrained among a group of migrant workers that an audience of 1,000 men broke into cheers when the male character in an anti-HIV street play hit his wife for suggesting that he use a condom.

## VOLUNTARY COUNSELING AND TESTING

In some places women's fear of men's reaction has kept them away from voluntary HIV/AIDS counseling and testing. This reticence has implications both for controlling sexual transmission of the virus and for efforts to reduce mother-to-child transmission.

Health professionals have only recently begun to consider the implications of encouraging women to reveal HIV infection to their partners. Concerned that many infected women were not sharing their test results with their partners, researchers in Nairobi began to explore why. Among 243 women, only 66 disclosed their status to their partners. Of these 66 women, at least 11 had been chased away from home or replaced by another wife, 7 had been beaten up by their partners, and one had committed suicide, according to spontaneous reports by the women or their relatives.

In response, the study team revised its protocol to allow women to decide voluntarily whether to receive their results and to counsel women on the possible risks and benefits of disclosure to an intimate partner. As a result, reports of violence diminished markedly in the next year, with no drop in the percentage of partners counseled.

In the US findings have been mixed on the impact of fear of violence on women's willingness to be tested for HIV. Fear of violence was not a dominant factor in women's decision to decline an HIV test among women attending STD clinics in Miami or Newark.

Nearly one woman in every six reported partner violence in the past year, but victims were no more likely than others to decline a test, except among women who had been injured by their partner within the past 12 months.

Other studies, however, find that the fear of violence is a serious concern for some women, suggesting that domestic violence should be considered when formulating partner notification policies and in HIV counseling. In a US survey of 136 providers of HIV-related care, 24% reported having at least one female patient who experienced physical violence after disclosing her HIV status to her partner, and 45% had patients who feared such a reaction.

### *Reducing Perinatal Transmission*

Fear of violence has also interfered with efforts to reduce mother-to-child transmission of HIV. In a study of perinatal programs in six African nations, for example, fear of ostracism and domestic violence was an important reason that pregnant women refused HIV testing or did not return for test results. Elsewhere, fear of violence has interfered with women's willingness and ability to comply fully with a short-course regimen of AZT to reduce perinatal transmission of HIV. In Côte d'Ivoire only 3% of women studied took all of the recommended doses of AZT during labor. Researchers attributed women's reluctance to take AZT to their fear of revealing their HIV infection to friends and family, often for fear of violence.

Similar concerns have been voiced by HIV-infected women who have been advised to bottle-feed their infants to avoid HIV transmission. In areas where breastfeeding is the norm, women fear that using a bottle would brand them as infected with HIV, possibly exposing them to abuse.

## VIOLENCE LEADS TO HIGH-RISK PREGNANCIES

Around the world, as many as one woman in every four is physically or sexually abused during pregnancy, usually by her partner.

Estimates vary widely, however. Within the US, for example, estimates of abuse during pregnancy range from 3% to 11% among adult women and up to 38% among teenage mothers. Some of this variation is likely due to differences in how the questions were asked, how often, and by whom.

## OBSTETRIC RISK FACTORS

Violence before and during pregnancy can have serious health consequences for women and their children. Pregnant women who have experienced violence are more likely to delay seeking prenatal care and to gain insufficient weight. They are also more likely to have a history of STIs, unwanted or mistimed pregnancies, vaginal and cervical infections, kidney infections, and bleeding during pregnancy.

## ADVERSE PREGNANCY OUTCOMES

Violence may also have a serious impact on pregnancy outcomes. Violence has been linked with increased risk of miscarriages and abortions, premature labor, and fetal distress. Several studies also have focused on the relationship between violence in pregnancy and low birth weight, a leading contributor to infant deaths in the developing world. Although the findings are inconclusive, seven studies suggest that violence during pregnancy contributes substantially to low birth weight, at least in some settings.

In one study at the regional hospital in León, Nicaragua, researchers found that, after controlling for other risk factors, violence against pregnant women was associated with a threefold increase in the incidence of low birth weight. Violence in pregnancy accounted for 16% of low birth weight among the infants studied and posed a greater risk of low birth weight than such factors as pre-eclampsia, bleeding, and smoking.

How violence puts pregnancies at above-average risk is unclear, but several explanations have been suggested. Blunt abdominal trauma can lead to fetal death or low birth weight by provoking preterm delivery. Violence also may affect pregnancy outcome indirectly by increasing women's likelihood of engaging in such harmful health behaviors as smoking and alcohol and drug abuse, all of which have been linked to low birth weight.

Thus, particularly where smoking and substance abuse in pregnancy are relatively common, these behaviors may be the main ways in which violence in pregnancy reduces birth weight.

Extreme stress and anxiety provoked by violence in pregnancy also may lead to preterm delivery or fetal growth retardation by increasing stress hormone levels or immunological changes. Stress can reduce women's ability to obtain adequate nutrition, rest, exercise, and medical care. Stress resulting from abuse appears to be the most likely explanation for the link between violence and low birth weight found in studies in Nicaragua and Mexico, where smoking and alcohol use in pregnancy are rare but violence in pregnancy is common.

## VIOLENCE AND MATERNAL DEATHS

On the Indian subcontinent, violence may be responsible for a sizeable but under recognized proportion of pregnancy-related deaths. In India verbal autopsies from a recent surveillance study of all maternal deaths in over 400 villages and 7 hospitals in three districts of Maharashtra revealed that 16% of all deaths during pregnancy were due to domestic violence. In rural Bangladesh homicide and suicide, motivated by dowry-related problems or the stigma of rape and/or pregnancy outside of marriage, accounted for 6% of all maternal deaths between 1976 and 1986 and 31% of maternal deaths among women ages 15 to 19. The risk of injury-related death was nearly three times higher for pregnant teenagers than for non pregnant teenagers or for older pregnant women.

## VIOLENCE INCREASES RISKS FOR OTHER GYNECOLOGICAL PROBLEMS

Sexual and physical violence appears to increase women's risk for many common gynecological disorders, some of which can be debilitating. An example is chronic pelvic pain, which in many countries accounts for as many as 10%of all gynecological visits and one-quarter of all hysterectomies.

Although chronic pelvic pain is commonly caused by adhesions, endometriosis, or infections, about half the cases of chronic pelvic pain do not have any identifiable pathology. A variety of studies have found that women suffering from chronic pelvic pain are consistently more likely to have a history of childhood sexual abuse, sexual assault, and/or physical and sexual abuse by their partners.

Past trauma may lead to chronic pelvic pain via unidentified injuries, by stress, or by increasing women's susceptibility to somatization, the expression of psychological distress through physical symptoms. Also, sexual abuse in childhood has been linked to increased sexual risk-taking and thus to STIs, which can lead to chronic pelvic pain, often due to pelvic inflammatory disease.

Other gynecological disorders associated with sexual violence include irregular vaginal bleeding, vaginal discharge, painful menstruation, pelvic inflammatory disease, and sexual dysfunction (difficulty in orgasms, lack of desire, and conflicts over frequency of sex). Sexual assault also increases risk for premenstrual distress, a condition that affects 8% to 10% of menstruating women and causes physical, mood, and behavioral disruptions. The number of gynecological symptoms appears to be related to the severity of abuse suffered, whether there was both physical and sexual assault, whether the victim knew the offender, and whether there were multiple offenders.

## THREATS TO HEALTH AND DEVELOPMENT

The negative consequences of abuse extend beyond women's sexual and reproductive health to their overall health, the welfare of their children, and even the economic and social fabric of nations. By sapping women's energy, undermining their confidence, and compromising their health, gender violence deprives society of women's full participation. As a UNIFEM report on violence observed, "Women cannot lend their labor or creative ideas fully if they are burdened with the physical and psychological scars of abuse".

## Violence as a Risk Factor for Disease

Victimization is a risk factor for a variety of unhealthy outcomes. In addition to causing immediate physical injury and mental anguish, violence also increases women's risk of future ill health. A wide range of studies show that women, who have experienced physical or sexual abuse whether in childhood or adulthood are at greater risk of subsequent health problems.

Violence has been linked to many serious health problems, both immediate and long-term. These include physical health problems, such as injury, chronic pain syndromes, and gastrointestinal disorders, and a range of mental health problems, including anxiety and depression. Violence also undermines health by increasing a variety of negative behaviors, such as smoking and alcohol and drug abuse

Because most early studies on abuse and health involved women seeking medical treatment, their findings could have overstated the relationship between violence and poor health. But links between victimization and ill-health have been confirmed in recent studies among more representative groups, including random samples of women in the community and women visiting primary health care facilities.

One such study in a large health maintenance organization (HMO) in Washington State, US, found that women who experienced any type of abuse in childhood-whether physical, sexual, emotional, or neglect-had significantly poorer health than their peers. The study found that women who suffered maltreatment in childhood had more sexual and reproductive health problems, poorer physical functioning, more risky behavior, and more physical symptoms than non abused women. Moreover, the average woman who had been abused in childhood also had more diagnoses across a wide range of health problems, including infectious diseases, mental health problems, and chronic conditions such as hypertension, diabetes, and asthma.

Studies among women at HMOs provide good opportunities for examining the cumulative impact of violence on women's health because HMOs generally provide for all of their members' health care-including drugs, surgeries, doctors' visits, and hospital stays. Collectively, these HMO studies suggest three main conclusions about the health consequences of physical and sexual abuse of women:

- The influence of abuse can persist long after the abuse has stopped.
- The more severe the abuse, the more severe its impact on women's physical and mental health.
- The impact of different types of abuse and multiple episodes over time appears to be cumulative.

## Physical Consequences of Abuse

Not surprisingly, violence is a major cause of injury to women, ranging from relatively minor cuts and bruises to permanent disability and death. Population-based studies suggest that 40% to 75% of women who are physically abused by a partner are injured by this abuse at some point in life. The consequences of such injuries can be severe: In Canada 43% of women injured by their partners had to receive medical care, and 50% of those injured had to take time off from work.

In its most extreme form, violence kills women. Worldwide, an estimated 40% to over 70% of homicides of women are committed by intimate partners, often in the context of an abusive relationship.

By contrast, only a small percentage of men who are murdered are killed by their female partners, and in such cases the women often are defending themselves or retaliating against abusive men.

Nevertheless, injury is not the most common physical health outcome of gender-based abuse. Abuse may lead to any number of physical ailments including irritable bowel syndrome, gastrointestinal disorders, and various chronic pain syndromes. Studies consistently link such disorders to a history of physical or sexual abuse. Abused women also have reduced physical functioning, more physical symptoms, and spend more days in bed than non abused women.

## Violence Erodes Women's Mental Health

Many women consider the psychological consequences of abuse to be even more serious than its physical effects. The experience of abuse often erodes women's self-esteem and puts them at greater risk of a variety of mental health problems, including depression, post-traumatic stress disorder, suicide, and alcohol and drug abuse.

### Depression

Depression is becoming widely recognized as a major health problem around the world. The situation is particularly acute among adult women, who in most countries suffer depression at nearly twice the rate seen in men. Some researchers have suggested that most of the difference between the incidence of depression in women and men may be due not to biology, but rather to poverty, gender-based discrimination, and gender-based violence.

Women who are abused by their partners suffer more depression, anxiety, and phobias than women who have not been abused, according to studies in Australia, Nicaragua, Pakistan, and the US. Among women ages 15 to 49 in Nicaragua, for example, battered women were six times more likely to experience emotional distress, as measured on an international mental health scale, than were other women. Physical abuse was the single most important risk factor for emotional distress in this study, accounting for roughly 70% of mental health problems among women.

Sexual assault in either childhood or adulthood is also closely associated with depression and anxiety disorders. Most likely to lead to psychological disorders are sexual abuse occurring before age seven or eight, abuse by more than one perpetrator, abuse that includes genital or anal penetration, and abuse that is frequent or continues over a long period of time.

### Post-traumatic stress disorder

Many abused women experience post-traumatic stress disorder (PTSD), an acute anxiety disorder that can occur when people go through or witness a traumatic event in which they feel overwhelming helplessness or threat of death or injury. The symptoms of PTSD include mentally reliving the traumatic event through flashbacks, or "flooding"; trying to avoid anything that would remind one of the trauma; becoming numb emotionally; experiencing difficulties in sleeping and concentrating; and being easily alarmed or startled.

Rape, childhood sexual abuse, and domestic violence are among the most common causes of PTSD in women. The chances that a woman will develop PTSD after being raped are between 50% and 95%, according to studies in France, New Zealand, and the US. One study in the US found that the psychological effects of being raped were comparable to the effects of being tortured or kidnapped.

## Suicide

For some women the burden of abuse is so great that they take their own lives or try to do so. Studies from a number of countries, including Nicaragua, Sweden, and the US, have shown that domestic violence is closely associated with depression and subsequent suicide. Battered women who develop PTSD appear to be most likely to try suicide.

Women who have experienced sexual assault either in childhood or as adults are also more likely to attempt suicide than other women. The link is strong even after controlling for such individual risk factors as women's sex, age, and education and for presence of PTSD symptoms and psychiatric disorders.

## Alcohol and drug use

Victims of partner violence and women sexually abused as children are more likely than other women to abuse alcohol and drugs, even after controlling for such other risk factors as prior use, family environment, or parental alcoholism. In a survey among women seeking primary care, those who had been abused by their partners within the previous year were three times more likely than those not recently abused to be drinking large amounts of alcohol and four times more likely to be using drugs.

Do abused women try to blunt their reactions to trauma by dulling their senses with alcohol and drugs? Or are women who use alcohol and drugs more likely to live in ways that put them at greater risk of being abused by men? In the US a 2-year longitudinal study sought to answer this question.

The study found that woman who used illicit drugs, but not those who used alcohol, were at increased risk of being assaulted over the next two years of follow-up. As expected, any past or recent history of assault was associated with increased rates of alcohol and drug use, even after controlling for prior use and other factors. These findings suggest that increased alcohol use is more of an after-the-fact coping response to victimization, whereas drug use increases risk of being victimized at the same time that victimization increases the likelihood of using drugs.

## DOMESTIC VIOLENCE UNDERMINES CHILDREN'S WELL-BEING

Conflict between parents frequently affects their young children. Children who witness marital violence face increased risk for such emotional and behavioral problems as anxiety, depression, poor school performance, low self-esteem, disobedience, nightmares, and physical health complaints. Such children also are more likely to act aggressively during childhood and adolescence.

Children who witness violence between their parents often develop many of the same behavioral and psychological problems as children who are themselves abused. In Nicaragua children of battered women were more than twice as likely as other children to suffer from learning, emotional, and behavioral problems and almost seven times as likely to be abused themselves, physically, sexually, or emotionally. Among abused women in Nicaragua, 49% said that their children often witnessed the violence, as did 64% of women in Ireland and 50% in Monterrey, Mexico.

Studies in the US have found that in 30% to 60% of families where husbands abuse their wives, the children also are abused. Clinical experience suggests that this pattern exists in the developing world as well. While children's reactions to violence vary according to their age, sex, and the social support that they receive, children who both witness and experience abuse have the most severe behavioral problems.

Violence may undermine child survival as well. In León, Nicaragua, researchers found that the children of women who were physically and sexually abused by their partners were six times more likely than other children to die before the age of five. The study controlled for other factors affecting infant and child survival. One-third of all child deaths in this setting were attributable to partner violence. A study in the Indian states of Tamil Nadu and Uttar Pradesh also found that women who had been beaten were significantly more likely than non abused women to have had an infant death or pregnancy loss from abortion, miscarriage, or stillbirth. The study controlled for other influences on infant mortality such as mother's education, age, and parity.

While it is unclear exactly how domestic violence affects child survival, one explanation is that the children of mothers who are abused are more likely to be born underweight, a factor that increases risk of dying during infancy or childhood. Another possible explanation is that mothers with violent partners may have lower self-esteem, less mobility, weaker bargaining power, and less access to resources and thus are less able to keep their children healthy.

In rural Karnataka, India, a study found that children of mothers who were beaten received less food than other children did, suggesting that these women could not bargain with their husbands on their children's behalf. Similarly, 1998 DHS data from Nicaragua show that children of battered women were more likely than other children to be malnourished. They were more likely to have had a recent bout of diarrhea and less likely to have received oral rehydration therapy. They also were less likely to have been immunized against childhood diseases Figure 1.2.

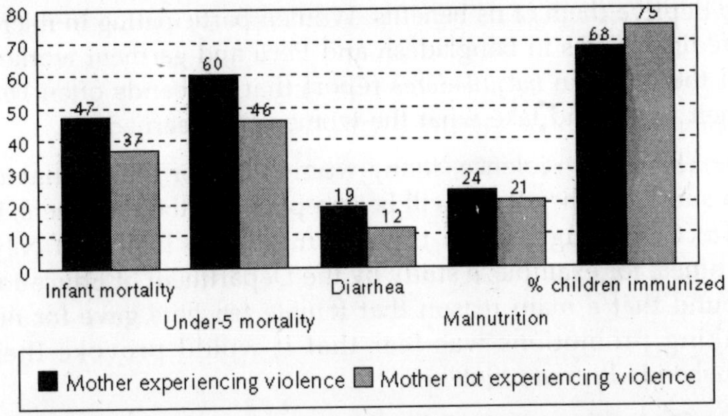


## GENDER-BASED ABUSE HINDERS DEVELOPMENT

In addition to its human costs, violence against women hinders women's participation in public life and undermines the economic wellbeing of societies.

Although techniques of estimating the economic and social costs of violence are imperfect, studies have begun to provide insights into the ways that gender-based violence undermines women's participation, reduces their productivity, and drives up costs to the economy, including medical care costs.

## WOMEN'S PARTICIPATION

Violence against women hinders their participation in development projects and lessens their contribution to social and economic development. In Mexico a study that sought to learn why women often stopped participating in development projects found that men's threats were a major reason. Men perceived the growing empowerment of their wives as a threat to their control and beat them to try to stop it.

In Papua New Guinea some husbands have prevented their wives from attending meetings by locking them in the house, by pulling them off vehicles taking them to the meetings, or by pursuing and dragging them home. Even if men do not prevent women's participation, they may use force to deprive them of its benefits. Women participating in micro-credit schemes in Bangladesh and Peru and garment workers in the Mexican *maquiladoras* report that husbands often beat their wives and take what the women have earned.

To avoid violence, many women censor their behavior to suit what they think will be acceptable to their partners, in effect "making women their own jailers". In Papua New Guinea, for example, a study by the Department of Education found that a main reason that female teachers gave for not taking promotions was fear that it would provoke their husbands to more violence.

Such fears can lead to adverse effects on the health of women and their families, as well as reducing earnings. Fear of rape, for example, has contributed to under natrition among Ethiopian refugee families living in Sudanese border camps. Ethiopian women refugees surveyed said they cooked fewer meals for their children because they feared being raped while out collecting firewood. In fact, many had been raped during the 2- to 3-hour forays to collect fuel. In Gujarat, India, female rural health promoters discussing obstacles to their work emphasized their reluctance to travel alone between villages for fear of being raped. They asked for self-defense training to continue their work.

## WOMEN'S PRODUCTIVITY

Researchers have only begun to explore the possible impact of domestic violence on women's labor force participation and earnings, and studies yield inconsistent conclusions. In studies in Santiago, Chile, Managua, Nicaragua, and Chicago, for example, the impact of domestic violence on women's likelihood of being employed varied greatly. Some women worked less in order to protect their children or because their partners would not allow them to work, while other women sought employment to lessen financial dependence on their abuser.

Domestic violence does appear to have a consistent impact on women's earnings and their ability to remain in a job, however. The study in Chicago found that women with histories of domestic violence were more likely to have experienced spells of unemployment, to have more job turnover, and to suffer more physical and mental health problems that could affect their job performance. They also had lower incomes and were much more likely to receive public assistance. Similarly, in Managua abused women earned 46% less than women who did not suffer abuse, even after controlling for other factors affecting earnings.

Evidence from the US suggests that victimization in childhood may also reduce a woman's educational attainment and income. Researcher Batya Hyman found that women who were sexually abused in childhood earned 3% to 20% less annually than women who had not been abused, depending on the type of abuse experienced and the number of perpetrators. Incestuous abuse affected income indirectly through its impact on educational attainment and mental and physical health status. Women sexually abused by strangers suffered an additional direct effect on income.

## COSTS TO THE ECONOMY

For countries the costs of gender-based violence are substantial. For example, in Canada a 1995 study estimated that violence against women cost the country 1.5 billion Canadian dollars (US$1.1 billion) in lost labor productivity and increased use of medical and community support services. Another study in Canada put the cost of violence against women much higher, after including costs for social services, criminal justice, labor and employment, and the health care system. The study estimated that physical and sexual abuse of girls and women cost the economy 4.2 billion Canadian dollars each year, nearly 90% of that borne by the government.

Not surprisingly, women who have experienced physical or sexual assault in either childhood or adulthood use health services more often than other women, as studies in Nicaragua, the US, and Zimbabwe show. Over their lifetimes, victims of abuse average more surgeries, physician and pharmacy visits, hospital stays, and mental health consultations than other women, even after accounting for other factors affecting health care use.

Such increased need for health care adds considerably to health care costs. For example, in the Washington state HMO study, the added cost associated with childhood abuse for this plan alone was estimated at over US$8 million per year. Another US HMO study found that female victims of partner violence cost the health plan 92% more than a random sample of other women who received services from the health plan that year. The extra costs were not due to excess emergency room charges.

## HEALTH PROVIDERS PLAY A KEY ROLE

Health care providers can play a crucial role in addressing violence against women. In most countries the health care system is the only institution that interacts with almost every woman at some point in her life. Thus health care providers often are well placed to recognize victims of violence and to help them. Moreover, because violence increases the risk of other health problems for women, early help can prevent serious conditions that follow from abuse.

Recently, the health community has begun to mobilize to meet this challenge. In 1993 the Pan American Health Organization (PAHO) became the first international health institution to recognize violence against women as a high-priority concern, when it passed resolution CD39.R8, urging all member governments to establish national policies and plans for the prevention and management of violence against women. In 1996 the 49th World Health Assembly followed suit, declaring violence a public health priority. Both PAHO and WHO initiated programs on violence against women in the mid-1990s.

Some health care systems have started to address domestic violence as part of clinical practice. In 1992, for example, the

American Medical Association published diagnostic and treatment guidelines for domestic violence and the US Joint Commission on Accreditation of Healthcare Organizations (JCAHO) began including an evaluation of emergency room policies and procedures for dealing with abuse victims in its accreditation reviews. More recently, Brazil, Ireland, Malaysia, Mexico, Nicaragua, and the Philippines have developed pilot programs that train health workers to identify and respond to abuse. Several Latin American countries also have incorporated guidelines for addressing domestic violence into their national health sector policies.

Despite such efforts, progress is slow. In most countries doctors and nurses rarely ask women whether they are being abused, even when there are obvious signs of abuse. Facilities that have established guidelines often do not monitor or enforce their implementation. US studies have found that few health care facilities have complied with the JCAHO requirements.

## Barriers to Addressing Violence

Why have health care providers been slow to address violence against women? Doctors often think that their patients, rather than themselves, constitute the main obstacle to better care. But health workers themselves often are part of the problem.

A complex interplay of professional, cultural, personal, and institutional concerns shape the ability and willingness of health workers to address domestic violence, according to studies in Africa, Asia, Latin America, and the US. Some of the biggest barriers that block effective response are health care providers' lack of technical competence, cultural stereotypes and negative social attitudes, and institutional constraints.

### Lack of technical competence and resources

Health workers often do not ask women about their experience with violence because they feel unprepared to respond to the needs of victims. Some view domestic violence as a private issue and fear that clients would be upset or offended if asked about violence. Others feel that they do not have the time or resources to help.

Practitioners who have received special training on violence are more likely to inquire about violence and to feel competent to address the needs of abused women. Although some professional schools are making efforts to address domestic violence-for example, nursing schools in the US -most professional schools worldwide do not address violence or do so only minimally. For example, a study in the US found that two-thirds of health practitioners had never received training on domestic violence. In Mexico and Zimbabwe health care providers said that their medical training was in fact an obstacle to dealing with abuse because it prepared them only to address a patient's physical symptoms rather than the whole person.

## Cultural stereotypes and negative social attitudes

Health care providers typically share the same cultural values and societal attitudes toward abuse that are dominant in the society at large. Thus they may think that some women deserve abuse or that a wife's obligation is to be sexually available to her husband at all times. They also frequently assume that domestic violence and sexual assault occur only among poor women or among women of certain ethnic or religious backgrounds. Such attitudes stand in the way of sympathetic and caring response to abused women who seek care.

For example, in South Africa a study found that female nurses generally recognized domestic violence as a serious problem for women but also thought that women themselves held attitudes and acted in ways that could provoke violence, including rape. Male nurses reported a long list of reasons that would justify a man in beating his wife, including if she disobeyed him, was disrespectful, or neglected household or childcare duties. They did not think that a man had committed rape if he forced his wife to have sex, and they thought that the practice of wife-beating was both a means of discipline and a way of expressing love or forgiveness.

Even in cultures where partner violence is considered unacceptable, negative social attitudes about battered women are often deeply imbedded and difficult to overcome. These beliefs may affect how health workers assess a woman's truthfulness or her responsibility for her situation. In the US, for example, clinicians revealed their biased attitudes by making such statements as "A battered woman tells you what you want to hear" and "Women in violent situations are difficult to deal with. We find it hard to accept women who don't get out of such a situation".

Some male clinicians may hesitate to accept a woman's account of violence because they identify with the offender. As one US doctor said, "Maybe my discomfort with it is that I've experienced that kind of rage myself". Female health workers who have themselves been victims of abuse also may have a hard time discussing violence with their clients. Studies have found that as many as one female health practitioner in every three has experienced violence herself.

## Institutional constraints

Clinicians working with victims of violence often feel that their institutions and colleagues value their work less than other types of clinical intervention. Most programs designed to address abuse in health care settings have been the work of very committed individuals, but their initiatives rarely have become institutional policy. With the departure of these key leaders, many programs lose momentum, and some end.

Legal liability or involvement is a major concern that keeps health workers from doing more for victims of abuse. In some countries health workers often refuse to examine raped or otherwise abused women because they want to avoid having to testify in court. Other countries have passed laws mandating that health care providers report child abuse and, sometimes, abuse of adult women. With adult victims, however, such laws are generally counterproductive because they take control away from the abused woman, jeopardize her safety, and may make it less likely that she will seek health care for fear that her partner will be arrested as a result.

Women's needs are often neglected because of bureaucratic gaps or inadequate coordination between the health and criminal justice systems. In some countries doctors are prohibited from treating women who have been raped or battered without authorization from the courts or police. In others, only court-appointed forensic doctors may examine crime victims. In Zimbabwe, for example, a woman who has been raped may have to wait three days or more for an appointment with a government medical officer. These officers are the only physicians authorized to document rape or assault cases. By that time time most of the physical evidence may be lost. Similar requirements exist elsewhere, including the countries of Central America, India, and Peru.

The lack of referral services and insufficient coordination between health workers and referral services often prevent women from receiving necessary medical care, including emergency contraception and STI screening. In Zimbabwe a woman who had been raped reported that, "The police said they could not file my case without a medico-legal exam. I went to the matron (at the health center). I was then advised to come to the (women's center). They sent me to Social Welfare. At Social Welfare I kept on being referred from one person to another the whole day. I went back the next day and was told to go back to the police station".

## Women's reluctance to disclose violence

Unless women are asked directly about violence, many do not volunteer information. For example, as noted in Table 1.2, the 1998 Nicaragua DHS found that over one-third of women who had been abused by their partners had never told anyone. Although 57% of the women had suffered injuries, only 13% had ever received medical attention. Even then, most women did not disclose the cause of their injuries. Only 7% of women reported having ever sought help at a health center or hospital for violence.

Shame was one of the main reasons that women in

Nicaragua gave for not disclosing violence. As one woman explained, "I thought that there were only a few people who lived like this and that it would be embarrassing for someone to find out that he was hurting me this way". Many women say nothing about violence because they fear that they will be blamed for it. A US woman told researchers that, even though her injuries often brought her to the doctor, she had kept their cause to herself for nine years.

Fear of reprisals from their abusers is another reason that many women stay silent. As one woman in the US observed, "I knew that if I was to tell them what actually happened, they would call the police and I would have to file a report, and they couldn't guarantee me that they would be there 24 hours to protect me from this maniac".

In much of the world women are unable to obtain health care without the knowledge or permission of their spouses or other male family members (333, 386). Women living in abusive relationships typically are subject to strict controls over their mobility, and abusive husbands may go to great lengths to keep them from getting help. Often, men will not allow their wives to visit a health center unescorted, especially if they are going to be treated for injuries due to violence. Women are especially unlikely to disclose abuse to a health care provider in front of their abuser.

## ASKING ABOUT ABUSE

Once a woman decides to seek help from a health care institution, the response she receives is crucial. Many clinicians fear that asking patients about violence and sexual abuse will open a "Pandora's Box," unleashing issues that they have neither the time nor the skills to deal with. When health workers fail to ask about violence, however, particularly when there are obvious signs of it, women are likely to assume that they are not interested. An indifferent or hostile reaction from health care providers reinforces a woman's feelings of isolation and self-blame and makes it harder for her to mention the topic again.

Lack of confidentiality can be particularly devastating, as well as placing women at risk for further abuse. A woman in Zimbabwe complained, "I went to the hospital because my husband beat me when I got pregnant. What hurt me was that there was no confidentiality by the doctors and nurses treating me. Everyone in the ward got to know that I had been beaten by my husband".

For many women, facing indifference and hostility from health personnel is like being victimized again by the very system that is supposed to help. One Latin American woman who went to a health center said, "I felt hurt, wounded, because when you go, you hope that someone would at least give you a little help. But when you get there you feel even more dejected.... They don't give you any encouragement.... They treat you like the cashier in the supermarket".

A Panamanian woman who miscarried as a result of her husband's beatings described her experience with the health center in this way:

When the doctor attended me, I explained to him what happened, that I had been beaten, and I said, "I know this isn't your job, but I need a favor. My husband is outside in the hallway, and I need you to call a policeman to help me stop him before he catches me again." The doctor answered that this wasn't his problem that I was free to leave however I wanted. He just said, "Take this for the swelling" and left me alone in the room.

"It is my impression that some women have been waiting their whole lives for someone to ask," notes Ana Flavia d'Oliveria, a Brazilian public health physician who began an abuse screening program among her prenatal care patients. In fact, most women, regardless of whether they have been abused themselves, feel that physicians should routinely ask their patients about abuse. Among South African women attending a community health clinic in Cape Town, for example, 88% said they would welcome routine inquiry about violence during health visits.

The way in which a woman is asked about violence makes an enormous difference to whether she will disclose her situation. If asked about violence in a nonjudgmental, empathic way, she is more likely to answer truthfully. Women are more inclined to discuss abuse if they perceive the clinician to be caring and easy to talk to, and if follow-up is offered.

Placing brochures or posters about domestic violence in a clinic or office can increase women's comfort in talking about abuse. Sometimes, medical staffs have found it helpful to wear buttons with the message "It's OK to talk to me about family violence and abuse." A US medical association produced a poster to place in waiting rooms saying, "We may forget to ask, but we always want to know if you are experiencing violence at home".

When there are obvious signs of abuse, such as unexplained injuries, health workers should ask, "Who did this to you?" If there are no signs, clinicians have found that the best way to ask about violence is to bring it up routinely as part of taking a clinical history. For example, the provider can say, "Because violence is so common these days, I ask all my patients whether they have ever been hurt by someone close to them." This phrasing can help to keep a woman from feeling that she has been singled out for questions.

Several short screening questionnaires have been developed to help health care providers identify victims of abuse. At one prenatal clinic, detection of lifetime violence rose from 14% with routine inquiry during a social service interview to 41% using the 5-question Abuse Assessment Screen. Another study found that asking three brief questions correctly identified the majority of abused women:

The questions took an average of just 20 seconds to ask, less time than measuring the client's vital signs.

There is no international consensus on whether all women should be routinely screened for violence when they visit a health care facility. Some advocates argue that failure to screen is a serious breach in the quality of health care. Others feel that screening all women on every visit may not be feasible, particularly where budgets are low and personnel are overworked. Some express concern that identifying women who are abused may be counterproductive if there are no services or resources to offer them and could lead to greater frustration for both clients and providers.

Each health service should decide upon a detection policy that best meets its clients' needs and local resources. Options other than universal screening include:

### *Ask When there are Signs of Abuse*

Without asking, it is difficult to identify women suffering abuse. Providers should keep in mind that, contrary to popular belief, physical injury is not the most common symptom of abuse in women. More common are chronic vague complaints with no obvious physical cause. Such complaints and other key symptoms raise "red flags" about domestic violence and sexual abuse that should arouse providers' suspicions. When one or more of these symptoms are present, health workers should ask directly about abuse.

### *Strategic Screening*

Another option is to screen all women for abuse in certain services that are considered strategic because of the number of abused women attending them, because special risks are involved, or because they present good opportunities for discussing abuse. Routine screening might be especially appropriate in the following services:

## Supporting Women Who Disclose Abuse

Health workers often feel that there is little they can do when a woman discloses abuse. But what providers say and do can have an important influence on a woman's course of action. The act of asking questions about violence can let women know that providers consider violence to be an important medical problem and not the client's fault. A Latin American woman said, "The doctor helped me feel better by saying that I didn't deserve this treatment, and he helped me make a plan to leave the house the next time my husband came home drunk".

Women in the US also emphasize the power of validation, noting that it provided "relief," "comfort," "planted a seed," and "started the wheels turning" toward changing their perception of their own situation. Some of the ways in which health workers can promote healing for women living with violence are described in the "Empowerment Wheel" used in violence prevention training.

Even if an abused woman does not disclose the violence on a first visit, asking about it shows that the clinician cares, and thus she may decide to talk about it later. While health workers ideally should coordinate their actions with community-based services, such as local women's groups, providers can take several useful actions immediately during the clinic visit:

1. Assess for immediate danger. Find out whether the woman feels that she or her children are in immediate danger. If so, help her consider various courses of action. Is there a friend or relative who can help her? If there is a women's shelter or a crisis center in the area, offer to make contact. Some hospitals and clinics have adopted explicit policies allowing abused women to be admitted overnight if it is unsafe for them to return home. Leaving a violent partner temporarily does not necessarily end the violence, however. The most dangerous moment for a woman with an abusive partner is often immediately after she leaves or decides to leave a relationship.
2. Provide appropriate care. For women who have suffered sexual assault, appropriate care may include providing emergency contraception and presumptive treatment for gonnorhea, syphilis, or other locally prevalent STIs. Unless clearly necessary, clinicians should avoid prescribing tranquilizers and mood-altering drugs to women who are living with an abusive partner since these may impair their ability to predict and react to their partners' attacks.
3. Document women's condition. Few providers adequately document cases of abuse against women. In Johannesburg,

South Africa, a review found that in 78% of cases of abuse providers had not recorded the identity of the perpetrator. Clinical records included such graphic but general descriptions as "chopped with an axe" or "stabbed with a knife".

Careful documentation of a woman's symptoms or injuries, as well as her history of abuse, is helpful for future medical follow-up. Documentation is also important in the event that she decides to press charges against the abuser or to seek custody of children. Documentation should be as thorough as possible and clearly state the identity of the offender and his or her relationship to the victim.

4. Develop a safety plan. Although women cannot prevent violence from recurring, and they may not be ready to report their partner to the police, there are ways that they can protect themselves and their children. These include keeping a bag packed with important documents, keys, and a change of clothes, or developing a signal to let children know they need to seek help from neighbors. Health care providers should review a sample safety plan with the woman and decide together which actions may help in her situation. Sample safety plans can also be taped to clinic bathroom and examining room walls, where women can read them without embarrassment.
5. Inform women of their rights. When a woman takes the step of disclosing her situation, it is crucial that medical practitioners reaffirm that the violence is not her fault and that no one deserves to be beaten or raped. The penal codes of most countries criminalize rape and physical assault, even if specific laws against domestic violence do not exist. Medical staff should find out what legal protections exist for victims of abuse and where women and children can turn for genuine help in enforcing their rights.
6. Refer women to community resources. Health care providers can help victims of abuse by identifying them early and referring them to available local resources. The needs of victims generally extend beyond what the health

sector alone can provide. Therefore it is essential that health care providers know in advance what other resources are available to help victims of abuse. It is especially useful for health workers to meet personally with others who provide services for victims of violence because a provider will be more likely to refer a woman to someone whom they know-when there is a face behind the name.

## Moving Outside the Clinic

To address violence against women, it is important for health care programs to move outside the clinic. Most health programs engage in community activities. Some of these can be mobilized to address abuse. Especially important is addressing gender inequity and abuse through community health promotion activities and mass-media campaigns.

### *Community Health Promotion*

For years health projects have used community outreach and peer education techniques to promote family planning, oral re hydration therapy, and other healthy behavior. Such techniques also can address the problem of violence-for example, by challenging harmful traditional gender norms and promoting new norms.

For example, the Mexican Family Planning Association (MEXFAM) has begun integrating antiviolence work into all of its programming. With funding from the MacArthur Foundation, MEXFAM has produced posters and workshop materials that encourage rural and indigenous men and women, including young people, to reflect upon domestic violence and its negative impacts. The goal is to help men and women begin to recognize the costs of abusive behavior and thereby become more motivated to change it.

In Honduras the Programa Feminina Hondureña de Salud Comunitaria (PROFEHSAC) has added drama, discussion, and role-playing on domestic violence to its training program for health promoters. As a result, PROFESHSAC health promoters have become major agents of change in their community, offering support to victims and holding discussion sessions with men, women, and youth.

The new popular education manual, *Where Women Have No Doctor*, should greatly facilitate such work because it features entire chapters on sexuality, domestic violence, mental health, and rape. Designed for low-literacy populations, this resource manual includes basic information on the dynamics of abuse and suggests how community health workers can assist victims and work to change cultural norms.

Programs also can include gender and violence themes in small-group sessions designed for other purposes. An example is Stepping Stones, a curriculum for sexual health and HIV prevention. Building on the pioneering work of two Brazilians-educator Paolo Freire and theater director and social activist Augusto Boal-the curriculum uses a problem posing approach to encourage reflection on complex issues such as trust, risk, the meaning of love, and learning to say "no". A recent South African adaptation of the Stepping Stones curriculum adds a module specifically to address abuse and coercion in relationships.

### *Communication Campaigns*

Reproductive health programs also can use the mass media to address violence against women. During the 1990s, for example, a network of over 100 women's organizations in Nicaragua mounted an annual mass-media campaign to raise awareness of the impact of violence on women. Using slogans such as "Quiero vivir sin violencia" (I want to live without violence), the campaign mobilized communities against abuse. According to the 1998 DHS, more than half of the Nicaraguan population had heard at least one of the campaign's messages, and one-half of all women who had heard the messages were able to repeat at least one of the slogans.

Another Nicaraguan organization, Puntos de Encuentro, recently mounted a campaign specifically to reach men. The campaign built on the results of an in-depth qualitative study designed to explore what benefits, if any, nonviolent men perceived from their nonviolence.

Another innovative communication program in Western Australia used radio and television spots to encourage abusive men to seek help voluntarily by calling a Men's Domestic Violence Helpline. The Helpline offers phone counseling and refers men to free, government-sponsored treatment programs. After only 7 months, 69% of adult men in the general population were aware of the helpline for abusive men, and 1,385 men had called, including 867 self-admitted batterers, almost half of whom accepted a referral for counseling.

Reproductive health programs also can ensure that communication campaigns do not inadvertently reinforce negative gender roles or deliver negative messages about gender-based abuse. The imagery used in campaigns helps shape how people think and behave. Campaigns that seek to promote contraceptives or condoms specifically by appealing to macho imagery, for example, run the risk of reinforcing negative male stereotypes that undermine women's power within sexual relationships. The Jamaican marketing campaign for *Slam* condoms, for example, used explicit references to rough sex and pictures of scantily clad dance hall girls to promote condom use to men.

Similarly, evaluation of *Hum Log (We the People)*, India's first television soap opera designed to promote social themes, found that its plot inadvertently reinforced domestic violence. Characters intended to be positive role models did not consistently benefit from treating women better, while the negative role models were not consistently punished for treating women poorly. Many viewers of the program praised the long-suffering woman who accepted abuse from her husband and noted that she kept peace in her family, thus benefiting from her self-effacing behavior.

In contrast, the South African television drama "Soul City" successfully used entertainment media to challenge attitudes and norms that perpetuate abuse. This prime-time television drama weaves social responsibility themes concerning sexual coercion, harassment, and domestic violence into its stories.

In addition, the program collaborates with the National Network on Violence against Women to provide a toll-free hotline and free counseling services for victims of violence. "Once people can witness their own situations on television, and watch the characters they relate to solve their problems, they are empowered to take action in their own lives," said Soul City researcher Thuli Shongwe.

## AN AGENDA FOR CHANGE

Ending violence against women requires strategies coordinated among many sectors of society and at community and national levels. In some countries reproductive health programs have taken the lead in addressing violence against women. But efforts must go far beyond the health sector alone. An agenda for change must include: empowering women and girls; raising the costs to abusers; providing for the needs of victims; coordinating institutional and individual responses; involving youth; reaching out to men; and changing community norms.

### EMPOWERING WOMEN AND GIRLS

Empowering women and girls is not only a worthy goal in its own right but also a key strategy for eliminating violence. Women will never escape violence as long as they are financially dependent on men and derive their social value exclusively from their role as wife and mother. Legal codes and customary practices in many parts of the world still treat women as second-class citizens, denying them the right to own property, to travel freely, and to gain access to economic and productive resources. In virtually all countries women are underrepresented in positions of leadership, and their specific concerns are rarely reflected in public policy. As a result, women frequently lack the power necessary to make basic decisions and informed choices about their own health or sexuality.

Empowerment is generally viewed as a long-term process, occurring at the international, national, community, and individual level. Its goals are to:

- Eliminate laws that discriminate against women and children,
- Strengthen women in leadership and decision-making,
- Increase access to education for women and girls,
- Increase women's access to and control over economic resources,
- Increase women's access to health information and women's control over their own bodies,
- Improve women's self-esteem and sense of personal power.

Worldwide, networks of women's groups are working to achieve these goals through grassroots activism and lobbying at a political level to change discriminatory policies and practices. Women's organizing has achieved some impressive gains. For example, in the last decade 24 Latin American and Caribbean countries have reformed laws related to domestic violence, largely due to pressure from women's groups.

In addition, thousands of NGOs are working to instill a greater sense of entitlement among women via human rights education, legal literacy programs, gender training, and other small-group efforts. In Nepal, for example, the Asia Foundation sponsored human rights workshops in 1998 for 90,000 rural women to educate them about their rights and to encourage collective action. In the Muslim world the Sisterhood Is Global Institute runs similar workshops for women. Their manual, *Safe and Secure: Eliminating Violence against Women in Muslim Societies,* uses case studies to spark discussion of issues such as child marriage, honor killings, and spousal violence. According to the institute, "Women must reclaim and re-interpret their culture in order to reach the goal of self-empowerment".

## RAISING THE COSTS TO ABUSERS

Research in the US shows that rates of interpersonal violence decrease in response to policies and laws that make violent behavior more costly to abusers. Western countries have relied heavily on the criminal justice system to achieve this goal, and in response to women's activism many developing countries have followed suit. At least 53 countries have passed legislation against domestic violence. More than 27 have enacted laws against sexual harassment, and 41 now regard marital rape as an offense.

Although such legislation varies, most laws include some combination of protective or restraining orders and increased penalties for offenders. Protective orders allow judges to remove an abuser temporarily from the home and to order him to seek counseling, to get treatment for substance abuse, to pay maintenance and child support, or some combination of these. If a man violates a protective order, he can be arrested and jailed.

In most countries, however, procedural barriers, gaps, and biases undermine the law's ability to deter violence and to protect women and children. Laws are enforced by male judges, prosecutors, and police officers, many of whom share the same victim-blaming attitudes of the society at large. Thus, as well as passing laws, it is crucial to sensitize police officers, lawyers, judges, and other members of the legal system and to help women know enough about the legal system to be able to insist on their rights.

In addition, many communities have explored other means to raise the costs to individual abusers of their violent behavior, such as public shaming, picketing an abuser's home or work-place, and requiring community service for offenders. Such practices presume that community disapproval can help deter domestic violence. As a Cambodian activist notes, "If a man feels that he will be severely 'looked down on' for battering his wife..., it is likely that domestic assault will decrease".

In the US state of Texas, for example, an innovative judge is sentencing batterers to "shame sentences," ordering one abusive man to apologize to his wife publicly on the steps of City Hall, for example, and another to carry a sign around a local shopping mall that read, "I went to jail for assaulting my wife. This could be you". Similarly, Indian activists often stage *dharnas*, a form of public shaming and protest, in front of the house or workplace of abusive men.

## PROVIDING FOR THE NEEDS OF VICTIMS

The needs of victims are complex. A woman in crisis needs physical safety, emotional support, and assistance in resolving such issues as child support, custody, and employment. If she chooses to press legal charges against her abuser, she also needs help negotiating police and court procedures. Often, what she needs most is a safe, supportive environment in which to explore her options and decide what to do next.

In many countries advocates have responded by setting up crisis centers or other services to address the many needs of abused women and girls. Such centers generally offer medical, legal, and counseling services, often all in one location. Some services are funded and run by government, and others, by women's organizations or other nonprofit groups.

Services run by women's groups have pioneered the use of support groups and nondirective feminist counseling designed to empower women. Support groups can play an important role in reducing women's sense of isolation, allowing them to develop a common understanding of violence and to share coping strategies.

Developed countries often have relied on shelters to protect women in crisis. Shelters are costly to maintain, however, and require women to uproot themselves and their children just when familiar surroundings and continuity in schools and friendships could be a great support.

Communities are now experimenting with other low-cost ways to increase women's safety, such as providing safe home networks and sanctuary churches where women can seek safety and support. In industrial countries such as Sweden and the US, municipal governments and private companies have tried providing battered women with cellular phones, alarm devices, and even guard dogs to help protect them from abusive partners.

Elsewhere, governments have experimented with police stations staffed only by women-an innovation that began in Brazil and has now spread throughout Latin America and parts of Asia. Although good in theory, such efforts to date have faced many problems, evaluations show.

While the presence of a women's police station increases the number of abused women coming forward, frequently the women require services-such as legal advice and emotional counseling-that are not available at the stations. Moreover, the assumption that female officers will be more sympathetic to victims has not always proved true. Female officers assigned to all-women stations frequently have been ridiculed by their peers and have become demoralized. To be viable, this strategy must be accompanied by sensitivity training for officers, mechanisms to reward and legitimate the work, and provision of a wider array of services.

## COORDINATING INSTITUTIONAL AND INDIVIDUAL RESPONSES

In most countries women have to overcome many institutional barriers to get the help they need. There is little coordination among the many institutions with which abuse victims interact, such as health care, child welfare, and law enforcement agencies. Even worse, when victims seek help, some of these agencies tend to be unresponsive or even hostile.

Institutions at all levels of the health care delivery system and in the community can best respond to the needs of abused women if they are trained and organized to do so. The appropriate types of response depend on the level and staffing of the institution Table 1.6. People not only in health care but in other areas as well-including community and religious leaders, the mass media, and parents-can promote nonviolent relationships.

**Table 1.6. Applying Communication Strategies to Address Violence Communication Focus for Different Audiences**

| *Strategies for Clients/Community Members* | *Strategies for Health Care Products* |
|---|---|
| ***When Audience Is Adults*** | |
| Conduct workshops and campaigns to de-legitimize violence as a way to resolve conflict or to "discipline" women or children.<br><br>Highlight the prevalence of abuse and its costs to families and society (e.g., impact of witnessing violence in childhood).<br><br>Promote supportive responses (not blaming) to victims of physical or sexual abuse, using street theater, alternative media, and public education campaigns.<br><br>Integrate plot lines about physical and sexual abuse into TV and radio programming, especially into social dramas produced to promote reproductive health.<br><br>Ensure that all media projects produced to promote family planning or other health goals promote gender equity by portraying competent women and caring men.<br><br>Conduct health campaigns to discourage use of alcohol and drugs.<br><br>Promote human rights education and other ways to empower women. | Stress key role that health care providers can play in early detection, treatment, and referral of victims of violence.<br><br>Educate providers on the long term health consequences of physical and sexual abuse.<br><br>Promote an ethic of care so that providers see themselves as responsible for the whole person, not just the person's symptoms. |

| *When Audience Is Children* | |
|---|---|
| Promote life-skills training in Schools and out-of-school settings; include age-appropriate content on Sexuality, conflict resolution, building healthy relationships, and personal safety.<br><br>Initiate specialized campaigns to prevent violence, e.g., "Hands are not for hitting." | Alert providers to the prevalence and epidemiology of child abuse, including sexual abuse.<br><br>Educate providers on the long-term consequences of early abuse, both sexual and nonsexual.<br><br>Encourage providers to promote nonphysical forms of child discipline. |
| *When Audience Is Adolescents* | |
| Provide comprehensive sexuality education including exercises that examine gender norms, double standards for male and female sexual behavior; role-playing on resisting pressure to engage in unwanted sexual behavior.<br><br>Enable boys and girls (first separately, then in mixed groups) to discuss relationships, love, anger, jealousy, and abuse. Educate young women about | Alert providers to the high possibility of sexual abuse in cases of STI or pregnancy in girls under age 14.<br><br>Help providers confront their own attitudes toward adolescent sexuality, proper gender roles, and victims of rape or abuse. |

*Prepared by the Center for Health and Gender Equity (CHANGE) for Population Reports.*

Many countries have developed national and local plans to improve coordination between public officials and community advocates and to monitor the quality of services for victims.

The Pan American Health Organization has sponsored a project in 10 Latin American countries to explore how best to facilitate coordinated community action.

The project includes creating community-level coordinating councils, reforming the response of formal institutions such as the police and health system, and creating support groups for victims and treatment programs for perpetrators. A similar project is underway in six additional countries with support from the Inter American Development Bank.

## INVOLVING YOUTH

Social behavior is learned at an early age. Around the world a number of programs are working with young people to encourage nonviolent forms of conflict resolution, to challenge traditional gender norms, and to create new models of healthy relationships-for example:

- In Mexico the Instituto Mexicano de Investigación de Familia y Población A.C. (IMIFAP), a nongovernmental organization, has developed an experiential workshop for adolescents to help prevent violence in dating and friendship relationships. The workshop, called *Rostros y Máscaras de la Violencia* (Faces and Masks of Violence), uses participatory techniques to help young people explore expectations and feelings about love, sex, and romance; to distinguish between romantic and controlling behavior; and to understand how traditional gender roles inhibit both male and female behavior.
- The Ugandan magazine for teens, *Straight Talk*, focuses on relationships and stresses gender equity, positive values, and interpersonal skills. A recent edition entitled *A NO Means NO* uses a comic-book style to discuss sexual coercion and abuse. More than 115,000 copies of *Straight Talk* are distributed monthly throughout Uganda and supplemented with workshops.

## REACHING OUT TO MEN

Working with men to change their behavior is an

important part of any solution to the problem of violence against women. To date, most programmatic work with men has focused on establishing treatment programs for men who batter. Begun in the US, such programs have since spread to Argentina, Australia, Canada, Mexico, and Sweden, among other countries.

In the US the courts generally require men's participation in treatment programs instead of imprisonment for domestic and sexual abuse, although some men participate voluntarily. The content and philosophy of the programs vary, as does their length, which can range from three to nine months. The primary goal is for participants to accept personal responsibility for their violent behavior and to learn nonviolent ways to manage their anger and interpersonal conflict. Some programs attempt explicitly to confront traditional attitudes regarding gender roles and male dominance in relationships.

Only a handful of such programs have been rigorously evaluated. Evaluations suggest that the majority of men (53% to 85%) who complete such programs remain physically nonviolent for up to two years after treatment. But between one-third and one-half of men who enroll in such programs never complete them. Thus the proportion of all male abusers who benefit from treatment programs is small. Moreover, while men may refrain from physical violence after treatment, many continue other types of threatening or coercive behavior toward their partners. Nevertheless, a recent evaluation of programs in four US cities found that most abused women felt "better off" and "safer" after their partners entered a treatment program.

Other recent programs encourage men to examine their assumptions about gender roles and masculinity and to become agents for change in the community. In the Philippines, for example, the NGO Harnessing Self-Reliant Initiatives and Knowledge (HASIK) uses gender training as a point of entry for organizing against violence in depressed areas of Quezon City. Men in the Talanay community formed a group named SWAT, for Support for Women Advocates of Talanay, to help men become better aware of gender issues. Members of the group intervene with the abusive husbands of women who have sought help at the local crisis center.

In some communities groups of men have come together to challenge male violence and to explore new models of manhood. Hundreds of men from Nairobi recently took part in a march to speak out against gender-based violence. "We are here to assert men's commitment to eradicate the customs, beliefs and attitudes that influence men to violate women and mete out violence against them," said Reverend Timothy Njoya, organizer of the march. Men's groups against violence exist in Canada, Nicaragua, Zimbabwe, and elsewhere.

## CHANGING COMMUNITY NORMS

Ending violence against women means changing the community norms and cultural attitudes and beliefs that give rise to men's abusive behavior toward women and that permit it to persist. Changing community norms alone will not eliminate violence. Nevertheless, it is difficult to make progress until there is a consensus in society that violent behavior is wrong.

A variety of norms and beliefs are particularly powerful in perpetuating violence against women. These include a belief that men are inherently superior to women, that men have a right to "correct" female behavior, that hitting is an appropriate way to discipline women, that a man's honor is linked to a woman's sexual behavior, and that family matters are private and it is inappropriate for others to intervene.

Programs designed to change these beliefs must draw people into discussion rather than alienate them by appearing to "demonize" men. To encourage people to consider new norms, programs have used such techniques as community theater and small-group work. In Cambodia, for example, the Project Against Domestic Violence sponsored a traveling theater troupe to encourage discussion about domestic violence and to portray models of new behavior. The troupe performed in 35 villages around the country and drew crowds of 5,000 to 30,000 people at each performance.

Laws can be changed and programs enacted that better protect victims of abuse, raise the social cost to the abuser, and influence cultural values. Perhaps most important, however, social attitudes must change so that women gain greater control over their own bodies, over economic and family resources, and over their lives in general.

Health programs and other institutions can help change the perception-often so deep-seated that it is unconscious-that women are fundamentally of less value than men. In the words of human rights activist Charlotte Bunch, "Only when women and girls gain their place as strong and equal members of society will violence against women no longer be an invisible norm, but instead a shocking aberration".

# 2

# Assessing Justice System Response to Violence against Women

## Introduction

For many of us, the adage, "there is no place like home" conjures up images of warm, comfortable, family scenes. For millions of women in the United States, however, this phrase has a very different meaning. For these women, home is a place of intimidation, fear, and violence. Domestic violence continues to be the leading cause of injury to women. In fact, women are at greatest risk of becoming a victim of violent crime in their own homes. The violence is not just debilitating - the injuries can be deadly. According to the 1995 FBI's Uniform Crime Reporting system (URC), 26 percent of female homicides are perpetrated by husbands, ex-husbands, or boyfriends (for those cases in which the victim-offender relationship is known).

Even if she is free of physical or sexual abuse in an intimate relationship, a woman faces the risk of being sexually assaulted by an acquaintance or stranger. Sexual assault is acknowledged to be the most under-reported violent crime on which national statistics are kept. Even so, the redesigned 1992-1993 National Crime Victimization Survey (NCVS) estimated approximately 500,000 women are the victims of some form of rape or sexual assault each year. In 75 percent of the cases, the victim knows the offender.

Stalking is another violent crime that plagues many women. Only recently have the justice system and the public recognized stalking as a distinct and serious crime, rather than an antecedent to other crimes. Beyond highly publicized cases involving celebrities and political leaders, there is still little understanding of stalking as a crime, and few people acknowledge it as one that affects "ordinary" people. In contrast to these highly publicized cases, the majority of stalkers know their victims, and much stalking occurs within the context of domestic violence, particularly when victims try to leave their batterers. A survey, jointly sponsored by the National Institute of Justice and the Centers for Disease Control and Prevention, concluded that one out of every twelve American women has been stalked sometime during her life.

Perpetrators of domestic violence, sexual assault and stalking discriminate against no one. Women of all ages, races, cultural and social backgrounds are victims of these violent crimes. The impact of these crimes extends to families, the workplace, and all of our communities.

Over the last two decades, dramatic changes have occurred in the public response to violence against women. Prior to the mid-1980's, the failure of the justice system to take these crimes seriously reinforced the escalating, recurring and often lethal nature of domestic violence and stalking. In this regard, the law - and those responsible for upholding the law - reflected society's tolerance of intimate violence, its prejudices against victims of violence against women, and its ignorance of the complexities of the issues implicit in these crimes.

In the mid-1970's, survivors and advocates gave voice to women who had previously been silent. The battered women's and anti-rape movements demanded additional legal protections and a full range of services for victims. By the late 1970's, a limited number of jurisdictions had initiated legal reforms. Some states passed new civil and criminal laws giving greater protection to victims and enforcing penalties on perpetrators. Criminal justice agencies, some funded under the Law Enforcement Assistance Agency ("LEAA") Family Violence Program, trained personnel, developed innovative policies, and modified jobs to comply with the new laws.

As research began to document the relationship between violence at home and violence in our society as a whole, the criminal justice system looked for ways to stop violence against women. Ongoing advocacy by women's agencies representing battered women and sexual assault victims helped communities understand an effective response required systematic and coordinated change, involving both justice agencies and community providers.

While an increasing number of jurisdictions have undertaken initiatives in recent years to respond to sexual assault and domestic violence, the efforts are sporadic. Laws protecting victims and holding offenders accountable vary, limited numbers of criminal justice personnel are trained to enforce the law, and only some communities have embraced a coordinated response to reduce violence against women with clear strategies for intervention.

## THE VIOLENCE AGAINST WOMEN ACT

In 1994, Congress passed and President Clinton signed the landmark Violence Against Women Act (VAWA) to enhance the ability of States and Territories (hereinafter "States") to respond to violence against women.

The legislation was designed to begin to close existing gaps and commit the Federal Government to an aggressive response to this epidemic. The VAWA creates new Federal laws, expands existing programs and establishes several new grant programs.

One of the grant programs was established as a formula grant program, designated STOP (Services, Training, Officers, and Prosecutors). The STOP program is administered by the Violence Against Women Grants Office (VAWGO), Office of Justice Programs (OJP), U.S. Department of Justice. These grants "assist States, Indian tribal governments, and units of local government to develop and strengthen effective law enforcement and prosecution strategies to combat violence against women, and to develop and strengthen victim services in cases involving violent crimes against women."

The VAWA defines violence against women as sexual assault, stalking, and domestic violence. It outlines seven specific purpose areas that can be funded with STOP dollars. It also requires states to allocate funds in 25 percent allotments in at least three categories (victim services, law enforcement and prosecution).

Understanding the importance of building a coordinated community response, the Act mandates each State develop a plan to implement the STOP program. The VAWA recognizes the key role community-based advocates have and must continue to play in developing effective strategies to stop violence against women. The Act stipulates each State must "consult and coordinate with nonprofit, non-governmental victim service programs, including sexual assault and domestic violence victim services programs."

## THE PROMISING PRACTICES INITIATIVE

In 1997, VAWGO, in cooperation with the STOP Violence Against Women Grants Technical Assistance Project (STOP T.A. Project), launched an initiative to identify and develop promising practices. This initiative is geared to help communities respond to the challenge of stopping violence against women. Thus far, expert panels have been convened to identify key issues and practices, a national survey of hundreds of practitioners was conducted, names and descriptions of over five hundred programs have been submitted, and in-depth interviews have been conducted.

In the spring of 1998, VAWGO will publish a comprehensive manual to help states and their sub-grantees draw on the most promising practices in their fields as they undertake implementation of the VAWA.

The manual will contain chapters on victim safety planning and practices responding to violence against women from the perspective of law enforcement, prosecution, the courts, and victim services. It will also offer a chapter on practices aimed at building coordinated responses to violence against women. Practice descriptions will identify a problem, explain how the practice addresses the problem, briefly describe the components that make the practice work, and propose an action plan to put the practice in place. The descriptions will highlight the barriers under-served populations confront when using the justice system and offer strategies to overcome these barriers.

Practices or specific elements of a practice will be illustrated by program examples. These programs will attest to the usefulness of the practices in saving lives, reducing violence, promoting victim recovery, and holding offenders accountable for their crimes.

In anticipation of the publication of the first volume, VAWGO is releasing the following assessment tool for jurisdictions to use in developing effective responses by law enforcement, prosecution, and the courts. The response checklists are not intended to be exhaustive; rather, they highlight some of the key elements of practices that will be fully explored in the manual.

Interspersed throughout the checklists are boxes defining the principles that undergird and enhance all of the proposed practices. The principles speak to the underlying values that should direct the design and implementation of any strategy to improve a community's response to victims of domestic violence, sexual assault and stalking. The values include: promoting the safety of women and their families; providing assistance to women to regain control and autonomy in their lives; and holding offenders accountable. These guiding principles of practice will form the foundation of the manual and are woven into the elements of the response checklists.

## UNIQUE NATURE OF VIOLENT CRIMES AGAINST WOMEN

The majority of violent crimes against women are committed against intimate or known partners. These non-stranger crimes differ significantly from stranger assaults in that the violence perpetrated against the same victim often continues and escalates over time.

In all instances of criminal behavior, the justice system seeks to apprehend and sanction the offender. In domestic violence related cases, the justice system must also take steps to prevent further abuse to the known victim, protect that victim, and connect her with community services which enhance her safety and well-being. The intervention by the justice system may be ongoing and change over time.

## AGENCY RESPONSE CHECKLISTS AND PROGRAM EXAMPLES

The following checklists describe the basic roles of law enforcement, prosecution and the courts in responding to violence against women. They also show where agencies coordinate and collaborate with other justice system agencies and community-based advocacy programs.

Review the following lists, checking off responses your jurisdiction performs with success. Make note of gaps in your current response to violence against women.

Also review the selected programs, which illustrate elements of agency responses and often utilize innovative and replicable strategies.

## INTERVENTIONS GROUNDED IN AN UNDERSTANDING OF VIOLENCE AGAINST WOMEN

Justice system personnel and community-based victim service providers can work together to develop and espouse shared beliefs about violence against women to guide policies and interventions. Shared beliefs should include:

1. Violence against women is a serious crime, requiring the justice system and community's attention.
2. No form of violence against women is acceptable behavior. Justice personnel must debunk the myths that overtly and covertly support violence against women, and replace them with facts about these crimes, the perpetrators and the victims.

3. Victim safety and welfare, as well as the safety of her children and other family members, is the paramount goal of justice system intervention.
4. Early intervention in violence against women cases, coupled with meaningful penalties and sanctions for offenders, can save lives and prevent further violence.
5. Responding to battered, sexually assaulted and stalked women from traditionally under-served populations requires multi-cultural services and multi-lingual capacity. Jurisdictions must strive to understand the unique problems faced by these victims and work with them to identify solutions.
6. Batterers, sex offenders and stalkers use violence to achieve and maintain control over their victims.
7. Victims are not responsible for their perpetrator's violent and controlling acts, nor do they have the power to change the perpetrator's attitudes or behavior.
8. Victims are in the best position to judge the danger the perpetrator poses to them and to make their own decisions about their safety. Practitioners have the responsibility to assist victims in this decision-making process by providing information about their options and available community resources.
9. The justice system must recognize the high risk of danger battered women and their families face when the decision is made to leave an abusive relationship. In many instances, domestic violence victims stay in the abusive relationship. The victim must be supported in her decisions, whether or not she decides to participate in the justice system.

## LAW ENFORCEMENT RESPONSE TO VIOLENCE AGAINST WOMEN

Law enforcement represents the entry point to the criminal justice system for a substantial number of victims and perpetrators. Agency training, policies and protocols can support consistent and effective police intervention in both misdemeanor and felony offenses, while connecting victims with community services and support.

Proactive and aggressive police response can deter further violence and ultimately save lives. Increasingly, law enforcement agencies are promoting early intervention in domestic violence and stalking cases to protect victims before more injuries occur. Officers are being trained to thoroughly investigate sexual assault cases, while being sensitive to the vulnerabilities of victims. Timely and responsive law enforcement intervention can increase victim safety, enhance investigations, and facilitate successful prosecution. Law enforcement intervention includes the following elements:

## Dispatcher Response

Address victim safety:

- Determine the facts and whether the victim is in danger or in need of emergency medical attention.
- If the victim is in danger or needs emergency medical attention, provide her with crisis intervention services and dispatch an ambulance, if necessary.
- Identify the crime as violence against women and give priority rating.
- Obtain information from the victim: name, address and phone, suspect's use of weapons, and whether the suspect is present (if not present, obtain description of the suspect).
- Promptly dispatch a patrol officer and backup unit, as necessary.
- Keep the victim on the phone until the responding officer arrives.
- Remind the sexual assault victim not to bathe or change her clothes.
- Record the victim's excited utterances.

Obtain offender history and information on the likelihood of danger:

- Use the agency database to provide the officer with any available criminal and civil history on the suspect.

- Furnish the officer with information on offender dangerousness and specifics about the incident.

## Initial Officer Response

Secure the crime scene:

- Respond to the dispatch call in a timely manner, whether it is an immediate or a delayed report.
- Evaluate the potential for violence and secure backup, if possible.
- Take precautions to ensure officer safety.
- Examine the area (e.g., listen for whether noises can be heard from within the residence, observe if lights are on in the residence or if windows are open, and look for evidence of children and the location of car).
- Enter the premises in compliance with the laws of the state.
- Immediately stop the violence and separate parties.
- Determine if children are present. Assess and respond to their immediate needs.
- Evaluate the scene (e.g., damage, alcohol/drug use, emergency mental health issues, or presence of other witnesses).
- Record the victim and the suspect's locations upon arrival.
- If denied access to the premises and forced entry is not appropriate, return to the scene on a frequent basis to observe any activity in open view.

Address victim safety and provide assistance at the crime scene.

*The following steps should be taken whether or not an arrest is made:*

- Assure the victim her safety is the priority.
- Inquire into the victim's need for emergency medical attention and provide first aid, if needed.
- Provide the victim with information on her rights, referrals to justice system agencies and community-based organizations, and assist with her immediate needs.

- Ask questions in a supportive and matter-of-fact tone of voice. Be calm, direct and patient. Be clear you want to help her.
- Let the victim know what her involvement in the investigative and court process entails.
- Notify the local domestic violence or sexual assault program to provide the victim with immediate assistance at the crime scene or elsewhere.
- If appropriate, encourage the victim to undergo a forensic medical exam and seek medical treatment.
- Explain to the victim the importance of evidence collection and medical treatment. Inform her the cost of forensic examination is not her responsibility.
- Arrange transportation to the designated medical facility for medical care and/or forensic exam, if necessary.

*Investigate at the crime scene:*

Interviewing the victim:

- Conduct the victim interview in a private setting, away from the suspect and, if possible, other family members.
- In the case of a sexual assault, or if there is need for emergency medical attention, conduct the interview after the victim has been treated (most likely at the medical facility).
- Obtain preliminary information from the victim about the crime and specifics leading up to the abuse, whether there is a relationship between the victim and suspect, prior history of abuse, any court orders, use of weapons, or use of alcohol/drugs.
- Record the victim's excited utterances and her emotional and physical condition.
- Note her demeanor, body language and other nonverbal communication.
- Document the victim's injuries and inquire about injuries that are not visible.
- Obtain temporary addresses/phone information from the victim.

Identify and interview witnesses:

- Identify witnesses and their relationship to the victim or the suspect (e.g., children or neighbors).
- Note the witnesses' demeanor and collect written statements.
- Interview children in a manner appropriate to their age, away from the suspect and the victim. Document any excited utterances, signs, injuries, or healing of abuse wounds.

Interview the suspect, if present:

- Obtain rough preliminary information from the suspect (let him talk).
- Record the suspect's excited utterances, his emotional and physical condition, and demeanor.
- Note the suspect's injuries in detail.
- Note any evidence of substance/chemical abuse.

Make an arrest decision:

- Arrest the suspect if probable cause exists.
- Where necessary, makes a determination of who is the primary aggressor, considering a number of factors (e.g., relative size of the parties, history of abuse, likelihood of future injuries to either parties, or actions taken in self-defense).
- Charge the suspect with all crimes arising from the incident.
- Decide to arrest solely on state law, and not on other factors (e.g., speculation the victim will not go forward, the arrest may not lead to conviction, or the race, culture, sexual orientation, class, or profession of either party).
- Arrange for the suspect's transport to a medical facility to collect physical evidence, if necessary.
- If the suspect is not present, obtain descriptive information (e.g., his possible whereabouts, the time he left, his vehicle color, type, and license). Broadcast the information to locate and apprehend the suspect.

- If the suspect is found, attempt to interview. If he cannot be found, apply for a warrant.
- File a full report even in the case of no arrest, explaining the circumstances.
- Explain to the victim the reasons for not arresting the suspect. Let both parties know the police take seriously crimes of violence against women.

Collect evidence at the crime scene:

- Assess the crime scene for physical evidence (e.g, fingerprints, body fluids, footprints, and/ or disrupted objects).
- Photograph and/or videotape the crime scene prior to touching, moving or disrupting potential evidence. Provide an indication of size or scale.
- Conduct a nondestructive search for all physical evidence at the crime scene.
- Collect, properly package and mark all evidence. Ensure all evidence is gathered before releasing the crime scene.
- Diagram the crime scene and document findings.
- Photograph the victim's injuries and alert her that subsequent bruising should also be photographed.
- Photograph the suspect's injuries and take full body photographs.
- Photograph children's injuries and demeanor.
- Impound all weapons used.
- Seize and ensure the 911 tape is preserved.
- Transport items requiring analysis to the proper crime lab. Store the remaining items in a secure storage area to properly maintain chain of custody.

*Facilitate the Forensic Evidence Collection Process:*

- Transport or arrange transportation for the victim to a designated medical facility for emergency care and/or forensic evidence collection, if appropriate.
- Make sure the victim is seen promptly at the medical facility.

- Make sure the victim has the support of a victim advocate, if desired.
- Confirm that the attending nurse or physician has a standardized evidence collection kit.
- Provide the attending nurse or physician with a brief account of incident.
- Photograph the victim's injuries or arrange for same-sex medical personnel to do so.
- Ensure all necessary physical evidence collection procedures are completed.
- Confer with assisting medical personnel to obtain further information.
- Request that the victim to sign a release of medical information form.
- Make sure physical evidence is collected from the suspect, if in custody (in a different location from the victim). The consent of the suspect, a search warrant, or a court order is required to collect physical evidence from the suspect. For suspect examination, brief medical personnel performing the exam. Provide general details of incident to help guide their collection of evidence.
- Make arrangement to deliver evidence needing analysis to a designated crime lab, and/or store other evidence in a way that maintains the chain of custody.

Write an incident report:

- Complete a written report, whether or not an arrest is made. If an arrest was not made, explain why.
- Include diagrams of all injuries, reports of injuries that are not visible, as well as information noted above.
- Report on previous incidents known to the officer or reported by the victim or other witnesses.
- Provide the follow-up investigator with all related reports and documentation, access to stored crime scene evidence, and lab findings from the forensic evidence.

## Follow-up Investigator Response

Address victim safety and support needs:

- Stay in contact with the victim, obtaining information and updating case status.
- On each contact, assess the likelihood of continued violence by the suspect to the victim and her family.
- Assist the victim with safety planning. Revise police response as needed to offer optimal protection.
- Work closely with a community-based advocate to support the victim through interviews and other investigation procedures.
- Encourage the victim to call the police if the suspect violates any existing court orders.

Gather further information to support charges:

- Consult with the responding officer (if different) and any officers who collected evidence.
- Develop an investigative strategy.
- Arrange for a subsequent interview with the victim if she was unable to proceed with a detailed interview following the incident, or if additional or clarifying information is needed.
- Re-photograph the victim to document changes in the appearances of the injuries.
- Encourage the victim to contact the investigator with any new information or evidence.
- Provide the victim guidance, forms and assistance in documenting the suspect's actions, if appropriate (e.g., to establish a pattern in stalking cases).
- Obtain statements from any witnesses not interviewed at the scene, identify additional witnesses (including "outcry" witnesses), and collect all pertinent information.
- Ensure all evidence has been identified, collected, properly stored, and processed from the crime scene, the victim, children that were present, and the suspect.
- Maintain contact with the crime lab to obtain results, and determine and respond to evidentiary issues.

- Obtain further information on the suspect's criminal/civil histories and other relevant background.

Identify and apprehend the suspect, if not already arrested:

- If the suspect was not at the crime scene and his identity is unknown, determine the most likely suspects. Obtain the victim's assistance in making a positive identification. Question the suspect once he is apprehended, using the appropriate investigative strategy.
- If the suspect is known, attempt to find and interview him, if possible. Also consider other ways to initially contact/warn the suspect, if appropriate (e.g., send him a letter of warning in select stalking cases).
- Arrest the suspect when probable cause is established.

Deliver the case to the prosecution office:

- Discuss the case with the prosecution office and secure additional evidence as necessary.
- Complete necessary reports and forms, and transfer information to the prosecutor's office.
- Testify as requested throughout court hearings.

## Develop a Victim-Centered Approach to Services and Programs

1. Make victim safety the top priority.
2. Respect the integrity and autonomy of each victim.
3. Maintain and protect victim confidentiality.
4. Regard survivor feedback as critical to improved justice response.

### Supervisor Response:

- Oversee officer compliance with agency policies and procedures related to violence against women.
- Oversee officer compliance with inter-agency agreements related to violence against women.
- Create forms and incentives to facilitate compliance with agency policies.

- Problem-solve with officers on complex cases.
- Assess whether police response meets goals of victim safety and offender accountability.
- Determine the need for additional officer training or supervision.

**Data Collection and Communications:**

- Designate and retrieve all case information.
- Automate case loads to expedite access to information.
- Track cases from first call forward, including case substantiation and follow through.
- Integrate criminal and civil history of offenders into agency database.

**Management Response:**

Set tone through the development of protocols, practices, training and other mechanisms:

- Establish protocols and practices grounded in an understanding of violence against women and embody values such as victim safety and confidentiality, respect for the autonomy of victims, and offender accountability.
- Develop police procedures for handling violence against women committed by law enforcement and other justice system personnel.
- Promote proactive intervention in all violence against women cases.
- Allocate funds, resources and personnel to violence against women cases.
- Support ongoing violence against women training for all new and veteran staff.
- Build a staff that reflects the demographics of the community it serves.
- Develop strategies to remove barriers facing under-served populations which prevent them from using the criminal justice system (e.g., translation of materials into relevant languages and 24-hour access to translation and interpreter services).

- Develop a system to monitor policy compliance.
- Revise policies and practices, as necessary.

Provide leadership in community initiatives to combat violence against women:

- Ensure coordinated response and collaboration with other justice agencies and other relevant service providers. Develop inter-agency agreements as appropriate.
- Participate in community task forces or other structures that respond to violence against women.
- Recognize and support community-based advocacy programs as primary victim service providers.
- Promote community education and zero tolerance for violence against women.

# 3

# Specialized Criminal Domestic Violence Courts

## INTRODUCTION

The National Center for State Courts surveyed courts by mail in 1998 and received approximately 200 responses indicating that the court had some type of specialized procedures for domestic violence cases. This article provides a basic overview of issues involved in the specialization of criminal domestic courts. To provide a framework for the study of these types of courts, this paper profiles the criminal domestic violence courts of Seattle, Washington, Sacramento, California, and Vancouver, Washington. These three courts are representative of four basic models for specialization.

## BASIC MODELS OF SPECIALIZATION

a. Model One: Pretrial Conferences Only

Example: Municipal DV Pretrial Court, Seattle, Washington

A "pretrial conference" is the court appearance where the prosecutor and defense attorney (or defendants) attempt to plea- bargain a case before setting it for trial. Some courts choose to specialize by having all pretrial conferences involving domestic violence crimes put on a separate court calendar. Other court appearances, such as arraignment and trial, are handled on the same calendar as any other crime.

Crimes without an act of violence to a person (such as theft), or without an easily identifiable "victim" (such as driving without a valid driver's license), are relatively straightforward to resolve. In contrast, domestic violence cases often require more time to negotiate than other crimes due to many factors: victim concerns, batterer intervention programs, consequences of a conviction on immigration status and firearm possession, to name only a few. In addition, domestic violence cases may require the physical presence of many more people than are required for other crimes: the victim, a victim advocate and/or witness assistant, additional court security personnel due to the heightened possibility of violence by the parties, and court services (probation) officers to provide sentencing reports on recommendations for jail time, batterer intervention programs, substance abuse treatment and contact with the victim.

Thus, courts such as the Municipal Court of Seattle, Washington elected to provide a special pretrial conference calendar for misdemeanor domestic violence cases. This allows the Domestic Violence Unit of the Seattle City Attorney's Office to schedule court appearances efficiently and to coordinate the use of witness assistants in the courtroom. Specialized pretrial calendars may make it easier for the victim to locate the courtroom and attend the pretrial conference if the victim wishes to do so.

From the court's perspective, a separate domestic violence pretrial conference calendar is the easiest type of court specialization. Unlike court appearances such as arraignments where the court must process all the arrested persons in a fixed time period, pretrial conferences can be scheduled to fit the court's staffing needs. During the time period from arraignment to pretrial conference, domestic violence cases can be easily separated from regular cases and receive the special processing required (such as attempting to contact the victims if this is handled by court services). A pretrial conference calendar happens in a fixed period of time (usually a morning or afternoon), unlike a trial or evidentiary hearing which may last many days. Thus, all three courts surveyed in this paper have at least separate domestic violence pretrial conference calendars as a minimum degree of specialization.

Profile: Municipal Court of Seattle, Washington

The Municipal Court provides a pretrial conference calendar for misdemeanor and gross misdemeanor domestic abuse cases.

Population: City of Seattle - 516,000

Court caseload: All crimes: in 1996, there were almost 19,000 non-traffic misdemeanors filed, 422 jury trials and 70,000 magistrate hearings. Domestic violence cases: in 1997, there were 5,359 domestic violence reports were received and 2,592 cases were charged. In 1998, there were 5,252 reports received and 3,536 cases were charged. In a typical month the Seattle City Attorney's Domestic Violence Unit will try between 10-15 jury trials.

Number of judges: In theory, three primary judges handle the domestic violence pretrial conference calendars. In practice, pro tem judges are sometimes assigned to hear domestic violence pretrial conferences as well. Number of court personnel: 210 full-time, 30 part-time employees.

Budget: in 1996, $15,757,000 for entire Municipal Court

Jurisdiction: Municipal Court hears misdemeanor (90 days and/or $1,000 fine) and gross misdemeanor (one year in jail and/or $5,000 fine) cases involving adult offenders. Civil orders for protection are heard in District Court and felony offenses are heard in Superior Court.

## HOW THE COURT IS SPECIALIZED ?

Misdemeanor domestic violence pretrials are handled on a court calendar that is separate from other misdemeanor offenses. The practical effect is that most pretrial conferences are generally heard by one of three judges who are assigned to those calendars, providing greater consistency for the processing of those cases.

The Seattle City Attorney's Office has a Domestic Violence Unit. DV prosecutors determine whether a domestic violence case is filed and provide bail and sentencing recommendations. Witness assistants contact victims and provide recommendations on bail.

Two DV attorneys and two witness assistants are present at the pretrial conference. One attorney serves as the "inside prosecutor," who remains in the courtroom and makes the court appearance. The other prosecutor serves as the negotiator, receiving input from the witness assistant and striking plea bargains with defense attorneys. There is an effort to keep the case with the same attorney, but it is possible that different attorneys from the DV Unit may handle the case at arraignment, pretrial conference and trial. The witness assistant generally remains the same.

The Municipal Court also has a weekly "review calendar," where domestic violence probation revocation, treatment status of DV offenders, and lifting of "no contact" order requests are heard by one of the DV pretrial conference calendar judges. The court specialization only applies to cases at pretrial conference. If a DV case is set for trial, it will go to the Master Calendar, and may be assigned to any judge on the bench for trial.

Calendar: In-custody arraignments for all misdemeanor cases (DV or non-DV) are heard seven days a week. Any judge or prosecutor may handle the appearance. The Municipal Court calendars special domestic violence pretrials all day on Monday and also Tuesday night at the jail. One of two judges typically hears the DV pretrial conferences. On Wednesdays the "review calendar" is held. The court hears DV cases concerning probation revocation, status of treatment for the DV offender, and requests by the victim for a lifting of the "no contact" order. The DV pretrial conference judge handles this calendar.

Cases set for trial go to the Master Calendar on Tuesday through Friday, where the case is assigned for trial to any judge on the bench. There are usually up to 25 DV cases for trial each week, divided among the three DV Unit prosecutors assigned to trial rotation. Only six courtrooms are available for the trial of ALL misdemeanors each week, so DV cases are competing for judge assignment against all other misdemeanors.

*Prosecutor's Office:* Seattle City Attorney's Domestic Violence Unit

*History of the DV Prosecutor Unit:* In 1978 the unit began as the Family Violence Project and consisted solely of advocates working for the prosecutor's office. At that time, any prosecutor could be assigned a DV case. In 1994, the unit combined advocates and prosecutors and a prosecutor was placed in charge of the unit.

*Prosecutor Jurisdiction:* This office handles misdemeanor and gross misdemeanor offenses (felony domestic violence crimes are handled by the King County Prosecutor's Office, which also has a specialized domestic violence unit). Most prosecutions occur under the City of Seattle Municipal Code, which mostly mirror state statutes. City prosecutors are specially deputized State attorneys so that they can prosecute under state statutes if desired.

b. *Model Two:* All Non-Evidentiary Appearances

*Example:* Domestic Violence Home Court, Sacramento, California

Some courts, such as the Sacramento, California Domestic Violence Home Court hear all non-evidentiary appearances for felony and misdemeanor domestic violence cases. Non-evidentiary appearances require legal decisions to be made by the court after arguments by opposing counsel and do not require witnesses to testify, thus they are much easier to schedule in a fixed time period. Non-evidentiary appearances can include arraignment (where the court determines the custody and bail status of the defendant), pretrial conferences (where the attorneys attempt to plea-bargain a resolution to the case without a trial), taking of a guilty plea and sentencing.

*Profile: Domestic Violence Home Court of Sacramento, CA*

*Description:* In July 1997, the Domestic Violence Home Court began hearing all non-evidentiary matters for all felony and misdemeanor domestic violence cases.

*Population:* City of Sacramento - almost 1.2 million (including fifth largest immigrant population in nation)

*Domestic Violence Home Court created:* July 1, 1997

*Court caseload:* In first nine months of specialized court operation, 3,225 cases referred for prosecution.

*Number of judges:* One primary judge handles the Domestic Violence Home Court. A second judge serves as the "back up" judge.

*Jurisdiction:* The Domestic Violence Home Court can hear both misdemeanor and felony criminal matters.

*How the Court is specialized:* All non-evidentiary hearings on criminal domestic violence are held in the Domestic Violence Home Court before one of two judges assigned to the court. This includes sentencing after a plea bargain (even if on the day of trial) and mandatory status reviews of defendant participation in batterer intervention programs. Only preliminary hearings and trial (which require the taking of evidence) are held outside of the DV Home Court.

*Calendar:* A typical day in the Home Court is the following schedule:

- 8:30 am Superior Court Reviews (pretrial conferences)
- 10:30 am Sentencing
- 1:30 pm Arraignment
- 2:30 pm Trial Status Conferences

Superior Court Reviews (SCR) are held Monday through Thursday and are the appearance where the vast majority of domestic violence cases are resolved within 30 days of the initial charge. If the case is not resolved, a misdemeanor case will be set immediately for trial, but a felony case will be set for a preliminary hearing.

*Prosecutor's Office:* Sacramento District Attorney's Office Domestic Violence Unit

*History of the DV Prosecutor Unit:* The current Domestic Violence Unit of the Sacramento District Attorney's Office began at the same time as the Domestic Violence Home Court.

*Prosecutor Organization:* There is one full-time supervisor, an assigned intake attorney who charges the cases, two lead attorneys (who handle 50% of the Superior Court Review appearances) and one attorney for Superior Court Review (who handles the other 50% of these appearances). There are also generally five trial attorneys, one prosecutor assigned to stalking cases, and one "threat management" prosecutor to handle Order for Protection cases and stalking overflow.

*Prosecutor Caseload:* On a typical day, the prosecutor will handle 30-40 cases at SCR. If a case is not resolved at SCR, the supervising attorney reviews the case and assigns it to one of the five DV trial attorneys to handle the case from preliminary hearing through trial. The trial attorneys typically carry a caseload of 18-24 cases.

*Witness Assistants:* The prosecutor's office employs four witness assistants (called advocates) who appear in arraignment and SCR. Witness assistants only appear at felony preliminary hearings if the case is a serious one.

c. *Model Three:* All Appearances in Specialized Court
*Example: Clark County District Court, Vancouver, WA*

Some criminal courts such as the Clark County District Court in Vancouver, WA, choose to specialize so that every appearance of a criminal domestic abuse case is held in one court from arraignment to trial and sentencing. As only the judges of the specialized court handle domestic abuse cases (in Vancouver, it is just one judge), this type of court promotes consistency of case disposition and expertise in domestic abuse on the part of the judges. This type of court requires extensive resources and a community considering this type of court must ensure that the court system (from probation officers to court clerks to judges) is prepared to adjust existing resources accordingly. The profile of Clark County District Court in Vancouver, WA, an example of both models three and four, follows the description of model four.

d. *Model Four:* Combined Criminal and Civil Jurisdiction
*Example:* Clark County District Court, Vancouver, WA

Much of the court system's involvement in the problem of domestic abuse takes place in family court and is a civil process, not a criminal one. Family court is the forum for seeking divorce, determinations of child custody, and Orders for Protection (OFP). An Order for Protection is a civil order issued by a court upon the request of a petitioner which restrains the respondent from committing certain acts, such as having contact with or assaulting the petitioner. (These orders have different names in different states, e.g. temporary restraining orders or protective orders, and different remedies are available in different states.) A violation of an OFP is a criminal act.

To obtain an OFP, the petitioner must prove that the respondent has committed an act of domestic abuse. The respondent may admit the abuse, or, if the respondent denies the abuse, the court may require an evidentiary hearing to determine if the abuse took place. Generally, counsel represents neither the petitioner nor respondent. After a domestic assault occurs, the victim often seeks an OFP in family court at the same time that a criminal charge is pending. This means that the court system is responding to the same act of domestic abuse in two forums: the family court and the criminal court. It is possible for the family court and the criminal court to issue conflicting orders about the respondent/defendant's permissible degree of contact with the petitioner/victim or regarding custody of the children.

Information about the same event from the same parties may be presented very differently in the context of an OFP hearing or a criminal court appearance. In a criminal case, the prosecutor usually provides the judge with the defendant's history. In a civil case like an OFP hearing, the respondent's criminal history might not be routinely provided to the judge. At an arraignment in a criminal case, the defendant has usually been arrested recently, and his/her demeanor may reflect the belligerence and level of intoxication/use of illegal drugs that was present during the abuse. In contrast, an OFP hearing is usually held days to weeks after the assault.

Some courts such as the Clark County Domestic Violence Court in Vancouver, WA, elect to combine civil and criminal jurisdiction in a single domestic violence court. The same court hears petitions for Orders for Protection and all appearances for misdemeanor criminal domestic abuse cases. This ensures that the judge is well informed about the entire situation and provides consistency in the court's orders.

The decision to combine civil and criminal jurisdiction in a single specialized domestic violence court is even more complex than the decision to create a specialized domestic violence criminal court. It has been only recently that domestic violence has been taken seriously as a criminal offense and not treated as "just a family matter." Combining jurisdiction in one court may encourage judges and prosecutors to focus on considerations inappropriate to their decision making in criminal cases. For example, judges, defendants and victims may all put pressure on a prosecutor to minimize or cease a criminal prosecution based on the defendant's willingness to pay child support or alimony.

Defendants have a Fifth Amendment right to remain silent in criminal proceedings and are usually represented by counsel. In contrast, parties in civil proceedings have no right to remain silent and the parties often do not have attorneys. Thus, combined civil/criminal jurisdiction may increase the possibility that a defendant's Fifth Amendment right to remain silent will be violated because defendants often address the court directly about the domestic abuse incident.

The problem of the defendant's Fifth Amendment right to remain silent can be addressed in several ways. For example, in Minnesota there is a statute that forbids the use of a respondent's OFP testimony in a criminal proceeding: Minn. Stat. 518B.01, subd. 15. However, there is still the potential problem of a judge who heard the defendant's admissions in an OFP context making decisions in the criminal proceeding based on any of those admissions.

Perhaps of even greater concern (from a prosecutorial perspective) is the possibility of the petitioner's OFP testimony being used against her/him in the criminal proceeding? In some jurisdictions the criminal defense attorney may represent the defendant/respondent in the criminal matter and at the OFP hearing. Because the prosecutor represents the State, not the victim, prosecutors do not appear on behalf of the victim at OFP hearings. This means that when the petitioner/victim provides testimony at the OFP hearing, the criminal defense attorney has the opportunity to cross-examine the victim without the prosecutor present. The victim's testimony at the OFP hearing may damage chances for a successful criminal prosecution because it will often provide impeachment material to be used when the victim testifies again in the criminal trial.

Although this practice does not raise constitutional concerns, it is still problematic for successful prosecution if a victim is cross-examined by the defense attorney in the OFP hearing while the prosecutor is not present. Combined civil/criminal courts may encourage the use of OFP hearings as a forum to cross-examine the victim.

Despite the potential problems of combined civil/criminal courts, Judge Fritzler of the Clark County Domestic Violence Court stated that combining the civil and criminal jurisdictions into one court was the "best single thing" about the creation of the court. Because of the combined jurisdiction, court orders about the contact by the defendant with the victim no longer conflict and there is coordination between victim advocates and batterer intervention program providers. Court Services Supervisor Chuck Bristol noted that the combined jurisdiction of the Clark County Domestic Violence Court helped "eliminate the manipulation" of the system by defendants.

Profile: Clark County District Court, Vancouver, WA

Description: The Superior Court agreed to give jurisdiction over civil protection orders to the District Court judge. Thus, the same District Court judge hears domestic violence criminal arraignments, pretrial conferences, sentencing, and civil order for protection matters.

Specialty Domestic Violence District Court created: 1998

*Population:* Clark County - 321,000, including Vancouver (population 128,000)

*Court caseload:* In 1997, 1,627 misdemeanor domestic violence cases filed, and almost 1,200 civil domestic violence protection orders filed.

*Jurisdiction:* Superior Court is the court of general jurisdiction and District Court has concurrent jurisdiction for misdemeanors and gross misdemeanors. District Court conducts felony preliminary hearings.

*Calendar:* Court personnel code the twenty-three types of domestic violence charges under Washington law. All criminal and civil domestic violence matters are available in the court file at first appearance.

- "Out of custody" domestic violence arraignments at 8:30 a.m. and "in custody" arraignments at 1 p.m. daily.
- Pretrial hearings and compliance reviews heard at 9:30 on Wednesdays.
- Domestic violence sentencing and show cause hearings at 9:30 on Thursdays.
- Temporary civil protection orders heard every day in morning and afternoon.
- Permanent civil orders heard Wednesday at 1:30.
- Jury trials are held Monday, Tuesday and Friday.

*Probation:* Probation officers are present at first appearance and attempt to contact the victim. If the defendant pleads guilty at first appearance, the probation officer is available to give an oral pre-sentence recommendation. Most defendants are placed on intensive supervision.

*Victim Advocates:* The City of Vancouver contracts through an independent agency, which provides services to victims and makes recommendations to the court concerning protection orders and release from jail. The County employs one witness assistant, as staff in the prosecutor's office, whose primary function is to ensure that witnesses are available to testify. The County employee does not provide information to the court.

## Reactions of Witness Assistants and Advocates to Specialized Courts

Each of the three specialized domestic violence courts profiled in this article have incorporated victim advocacy and witness assistance into the court's structure. Stephanie Avalon, a resource specialist for the Battered Women's Justice Project, contacted advocates and witness assistants from the three communities during the summer and fall of 1999 and asked them their perspective on the specialized courts. This section contains her summaries of those phone interviews.

Seattle Municipal DV Pretrial Court

Seattle's model is striking because of the number of witness assistants they employ and the close way they work with the prosecutors. Establishing the pretrial calendar facilitated the advocacy already being provided. Witness assistants have a strong role within the Domestic Violence Unit of the prosecutor's office, contacting victims and assisting prosecutors with case decisions.

Kristin Pugh has been working for the Seattle Prosecutor's DV Unit for about 3 years. She says the specialized calendar works very well for advocates, witness assistants, and victims because it makes it possible to have meetings with prosecutors ahead of the pretrial calendar, which would be harder to manage if pretrials were randomly scheduled. She believes the intense involvement helps to offset the tendency of overworked prosecutors to dispose of cases too readily. Without this assistance, the prosecutor would have much less information on which to base decisions.

At arraignment, witness assistants contact victims, convey information to prosecutors, and assist in making charging as well as bail decisions. Each witness assistant usually carries a caseload of about 50 cases at any given time. They continue to work with the victims they were assigned at arraignment. They make follow up calls to the victim and meet with the prosecutor prior to the pretrial. At pretrial, 2 witness assistants and 2 prosecutors cover the calendar. One team meets outside the courtroom to negotiate while another pair handles cases as they are called in court.

Witness assistants' files contain all the history of a particular defendant while prosecutors carry files of the particular incident. Information provided by witness assistants puts the individual cases in a larger context, allowing the court to see the pattern of abuse. This is particularly useful when a victim comes to court to request that a no contact order be dropped. Procedure requires that the witness assistant and victim sign a form requesting the dropping of the no contact order. If the prosecution team believes the no contact order should remain in force, the victim and witness assistant address the court. Depending on what the victim tells the judge, the witness assistant might point out the history of assaults, the level of injuries, or escalating control tactics as arguments in favor of keeping the no contact order. Kristin says that victims do not seem offended by this process because the specific information usually makes a reasonable and understandable argument.

Witness assistants can offer no confidentiality to victims because they work for the prosecutor. Kristin thinks this is only a problem if it is not made clear at the outset. Also, prosecutor based witness assistants cannot work with women charged with crimes, though they may have information about the history of abuse that could effect the charging decision. No clearly established referral system has been established to refer women charged to community based advocacy programs.

No community advocates typically work in the municipal court. Kristin speculates that they are serving different populations. She works with many Spanish speaking, low-income people who seem reluctant to use shelter and support group services, she says. Community based advocates work more in the civil arena. An advocate from a community-based program agreed that the population served was probably different, but also felt confident that victims were being well served by the witness assistants in the Domestic Violence Unit. With limited resources, community programs do not want to duplicate services. When victims are arrested and the prosecutor's staff cannot provide advocacy, the community programs will, she said.

## Sacramento Home Court

Carole Taverna works for the Sacramento District Attorney's Office as a witness assistant (called victim/witness advocates in this court). She described how the Home Court works, how cases are assigned, and the responsibilities of witness assistants from the prosecutor's office. A deputy district attorney evaluates all the incoming cases, judges whether they will be charged and decides whether the charge will be felony or misdemeanor.

Frequently, the intake deputy notes concerns requiring immediate attention. A special form was developed to advise witness assistants of those concerns. Prior to every court meeting, witness assistants attempt to contact the victim to provide support and gather additional information regarding her medical condition, what she might want from prosecution, whether substance abuse is an issue, and any additional information regarding history of abuse that could be relevant to the case. The information gathered is written up and provided to attorneys prior to the court hearings. Witness assistants are present in the Home Court to assist victims. Prior to establishing the Home Court, neither witness assistants nor advocates were always present in the court to convey their victims' interests. This alone is a large improvement for victim services.

An unanticipated problem arose in the Home Court when verbal no contact orders were issued, but victims were not always informed and enforcement was problematic. A procedure was established which provided that no contact orders were documented on a form which provides a copy for the court, the defendant, the victim and the prosecutor's file. The copy for the victim is usually provided in the mail. Now that a written record is provided, no contact orders are enforceable and violations do constitute a new criminal offense.

The primary advocacy program for battered women in Sacramento is W.E.A.V.E. Debbie Jacobson, Inter-Tribal Council of California, worked as a W.E.A.V.E. advocate for a number of years. She was involved in establishing DVERT, a program which pairs advocates with police officers to work on high risk cases, usually doing follow up work. In that capacity she was often in the Sacramento Home Court and able to observe what was happening. Debbie Jacobson believes community-based advocates should have been involved in the planning process to include battered women's interests that might conflict with the criminal justice system's agenda.

She named the number one benefit of the court to be offender accountability. With one judge hearing all the cases, the offender become familiar to the court. Carole Taverna agreed that the consistency of one judge seeing all the defendants is the best feature of the Home Court. With the calendar covering felony and misdemeanor, out of custody and in custody, offenders see and hear all types of cases. First time offenders can benefit by hearing a felony case sentenced and knowing that domestic violence will be treated seriously. The down side is that they also observe cases that aren't handled well.

The biggest pitfall in Sacramento, according to Debbie, has been that organizing the domestic violence calendar enabled the defense bar to strategize, too. Public defenders use plea bargaining time to access victims. They also began sending investigators out within a short time of arrest to speak to victims before the DA's office got a chance to reach them. Debbie felt that public defenders encouraged victims to come to the first hearing and primed them to say they weren't afraid. Prior to the formation of the Home Court, Debbie says the defense office did not have a uniform response and couldn't use investigators the same way. Cases were scattered throughout the court system, making an organized response difficult for everyone. So, while the Home Court enabled better prosecution strategies, it also facilitated the development of new defense tactics.

Witness assistants employed by the prosecutor's office provide advocacy. Debbie's opinion is that there is a role conflict which impedes the witness assistant's ability to effectively advocate for individual women and for system change. Carol Taverna described the duties of witness assistants. Besides being present in the Home Court, witness assistants accompany women to subsequent court hearings, and will assist them with victim-impact statements. In addition, witness assistants from the prosecutor's office hold a daily restraining order class to assist women in the filing of civil restraining orders. She says they work closely with W.E.A.V.E., which also attends the classes, and W.E.A.V.E. advocates are expected to go to the civil hearings with women who want advocates for that purpose.

Annette Lamber, an advocate currently employed with W.E.A.V.E. reiterated the benefit of a single judge handling the domestic violence caseload. The judge often recognizes offenders who re-offend with new victims. Annette thinks the Home Court is important because domestic violence is a different kind of crime calling for different responses. She believes victims are getting their needs better addressed because advocates are available in the court.

Vancouver Washington Domestic Violence Court

Shirl Zent is the coordinator of legal advocacy for the Safe Choice Domestic Violence Program, a program of the YWCA in Vancouver, WA. Shirl has been involved with the entire process leading to the domestic violence court, starting with the domestic violence task force which was established 8 or 9 years ago as part of a community commitment to address domestic violence more effectively. The task force was in place examining problems in the system for about 5 years before the domestic violence court was even suggested. After they decided to establish the court it took about a year and a half to get it set up. First the Protection Order court was moved from Superior Court to District Court, then the Domestic Violence misdemeanor docket was established. Now, they are involved in problem-solving issues that come up.

Shirl believes input from all related agencies possible is critical to the success of a dedicated court. Their task force included law enforcement, corrections, jail personnel, treatment agencies, social services, prosecution, (city and county) and advocates. Judges from district court and from superior court met with the task force at least once but did not attend regularly. The Washington State University provided an instructor and some students who helped with some of the paperwork and details of committee work. Defense attorneys were invited to participate, but did not really get involved.

Evaluations from battered women themselves have not been sought formally in any of these specialized courts. However, informal feedback from women Shirl has worked with over the years has been positive, she says. The system is more user friendly now and victims report the process is easier to use and they are feeling heard. For example, a problem developed regarding requests from women to dismiss the "no contact" orders issued when criminal charges were pressed. In a neighboring county, victims are told they must attend a 6-hour class before a no contact order can be dropped. Shirl thought this was inappropriate and burdensome for women. Shirl was being inundated with requests from women who wished no contacts dropped. She brought the problem to the attention of the prosecutor who informed the judge. When they met, a policy was established that no contact orders would not be dropped unless the victim also wanted them dropped and not until the defendant had completed his probationary requirements and requested a hearing before the judge. This has been working quite well, Shirl says. A few women who have had unusual circumstances have gotten no contact orders dropped with Shirl intervening on their behalf to the judge.

Shirl believes the success of their domestic violence court rests with the leadership of their judge. He has been very receptive, listened to problems, and included advocates in everything. That judge will rotate out in the next few months but the incoming judge is also very interested in the domestic violence issue. Shirl believes the leadership shown thus far has gotten the court off to a very successful start and improved communication with the rest of the bench. She is pleased with the strong, working relationship that has been established between herself and the judge and other court personnel.

## ISSUES INVOLVED IN SPECIALIZATION

### Advantages of Specialization

1. Accessibility for Victim-The more specialized a court is, the easier it generally is for a victim to access the System. A specialized criminal court may mean the same courtroom for all appearances, making it easier for the victim to find the courtroom. It means that key personnel such as the judge who sets release and sentencing conditions, the probation officer who makes release and sentencing recommendations, the witness assistant and/ or victim advocate and prosecutor are often available in one courtroom. Rather than the victim having to hunt for each office and service during a time of crisis, the services and appropriate personnel are connected to one forum to which the victim can be directed.
2. Expertise- Criminal justice personnel working in the area of domestic violence need expertise in the dynamics of family violence to understand the frequency of victim recantation and the potential lethality involved in the cases. In courts without specialization, judges often rotate through the criminal calendars, and may not have enough experience or training in domestic violence to accurately assess the cases before them. Judges may also be unfamiliar with the manipulative behavior of domestic violence offenders or the intense emotions displayed by domestic violence victims. Specialization allows judges to learn the unique characteristics of domestic violence and the resources available, promoting a more informed judicial response to the problem.

   Domestic violence cases often require a specialized knowledge of the law. Many jurisdictions have statutes or case law unique to domestic violence. Judges must have knowledge of the law pertaining to the admissibility of acts of past domestic violence by the defendant and the victim's out-of-court statements about the abuse, as well as special factors the court can consider in making custody and bail determinations in domestic violence cases. Court specialization promotes expertise in the law and the prompt, appropriate decision by the judge.

Court specialization often promotes expertise in all court personnel, not just judges. Probation officers, like judges and attorneys, may be unaccustomed to perpetrator and victim behaviors, and increased specialization may provide a context for appropriate release and sentencing recommendations. Court clerks assigned to a specialized court will also be more familiar with the dynamics involved and often be able to provide better referrals to victim resources. Court security personnel may be more alert to the potential for violence and the need to safeguard the victim in a specialized domestic violence criminal court.

3. Accountability
   a. For Defendants -As Chuck Bristol, Court Services Supervisor for the Clark County Domestic Violence Court explained it, the advantage to a specialized court is that "one judge sees all domestic violence offenders, rather than one offender having the opportunity to give six different versions to six different judges." Every judge (or probation officer) who sees an offender for the first time may give the offender the benefit of the doubt in release or sentencing conditions. Specialization increases the likelihood that a repeat offender will see the same judge and court personnel again-and that the offender will be less able to "downplay" or minimize the continuing violence.
   b. For Criminal Justice System Personnel -Robert Morgester, Lead Deputy District Attorney of the Sacramento City Attorney's Domestic Violence Unit,

> noted that the process of "consolidating in one court" all non-evidentiary hearings for domestic violence cases meant that the "problems in the system became glaringly apparent" and the attitude became, "let's solve them." Specializing the court meant increased awareness of the functions of different players in the criminal justice system and a commitment to address any lapse in services.

Accountability depends on strong lines of communication. For example, in the creation of both the Vancouver, Washington and Sacramento, California domestic violence courts, the process of bringing all the players to the table unearthed problems in the communication between batterer intervention program providers and the court system. Discrepancies existed between the perception by victim advocates and batterer program providers as to the reoccurrence of violence. In Vancouver, there are automatic court reviews of offender progress which the offender must attend at 60 days, 120 days and six months after sentencing. This practice has helped define expectations for the amount and type of documentation provided by the batterer program on the offender's progress (or lack thereof). These regular reviews have increased the accountability of the batterer programs.

For their part, batterer program providers got to voice their preference that the court provides the offender with specific instructions, rather than just referring the defendant to probation with a blanket order to follow probation's instructions. Thus, the specialization of the court increased communication between actors in the system and thus helped define standards to which the various parties would be held.

In addition, specialization increases visibility of the specific people involved in the various roles. Instead of a generic judge or prosecutor or victim advocate, the parties interact with each other routinely, typically creating strong relationships. If there is a problem with judicial or prosecutorial attitudes toward domestic violence, it will be harder to conceal. This, in turn, increases accountability.

4. Consistency in Case Handling - If the specialized court has both criminal jurisdiction and civil jurisdiction over the granting of civil Orders for Protection, that will remove the potential for courts to issue conflicting orders on the permissible degree of contact of the perpetrator with the victim. A specialized court typically means a limited number of judges who can draw on their expertise in domestic violence and render consistent decisions in factually similar cases. Victims can be given accurate information on possible judicial responses to the situation. Consistent sentencing policies mean that offenders can expect to receive increased penalties for increased violence, rather than hoping for the "luck of the draw" in appearing before random judges.
5. Timely Response - Specialized courts control the scheduling of domestic violence cases and thus control the time frame for prosecution of cases. Generally, the quicker the batterer is brought to trial, the more effective the prosecution is. Chuck Bristol, Court Services Supervisor for Clark County District Court, explained that the "closer you put the consequences to the act, the more they're [the batterers] willing to buy into treatment." The quicker the criminal penalties follow the criminal act, the more the batterer and victim will perceive that there are consequences for the domestic violence.

Victims are generally most willing to provide a complete and accurate report of the violence immediately after the assault. The longer the length of time from the assault to the day of trial, the longer the batterer has to intimidate or "sweet talk" the victim into changing her/his story. Specialized criminal courts can help speed the time to bring a case to trial and thus reduce the possibility of victim recantation.

Perpetrators of domestic violence frequently re-offend or violate "no contact" orders while awaiting trial. Specialized judges, probation officers and prosecutors make it easier for victims and victim advocates to get information to the appropriate personnel so that prompt action can be taken.

6. Message to Community - The mere fact that a court is specialized in the area of domestic violence can send a strong message to the community that the court takes domestic violence seriously. Clark County Corrections Counselor Beth Sharpe noted that "just the talk heard in the jail, now clients [defendants] are saying that the state can file charges even without the victim's cooperation and they know if they get a conviction that they will go on probation and get treatment."

## Disadvantages of Specialization

1. All the Eggs in One Basket- Consistency in a specialized criminal court is not a virtue if the personnel in a court make consistently bad decisions. Judicial tyranny or lack of competence is a much greater threat in any kind of specialized court than in a system where judges handle all kinds of cases on a frequent rotation. One commentator on specialized civil domestic violence courts explained, "The most notable [risk] is the 'all the eggs in one basket' conundrum: if the court is created and it doesn't work well, battered women have nowhere else to turn for legal protection."

   The problem of "all the eggs in one basket" exists well beyond the initial creation of the court. A court may start out well staffed and with excellent judicial leadership, but increasing caseloads or the departure of dedicated judges may lead to a malfunctioning specialized court.

2. Perceived Bias -The criminal defense bar may perceive that increased attention to domestic violence in the form of a specialized court will lead to increased jail time and penalties for defendants. There may be a perception that court specialization means that judges have become advocates for women and are no longer impartial arbiters of the law. As Assistant City Attorney Denice Biros of Vancouver, Washington, put it: "the defense bar perceives that the judge will hammer every defendant."

   Judge Fritzler of the Clark County Domestic Violence Court noted that judicial rules in the State of Washington prohibit judges from becoming a member of DWI or domestic violence task forces because it gives the appearance of judge bias. He chose to attend some meetings as an observer, not a member or participant. These sorts of rules and the perception of bias may hamper a judge's ability to organize and participate in the creation of a specialized court.

3. Increased Workload -Domestic violence cases, with the difficult dynamics of the relationships involved, the possibility of further violence, and the need for careful decisions regarding release and sentencing conditions, are very resource and labor intensive cases. Robert Morgester of the Sacramento District Attorney's Office explained that the creation of the Domestic Violence Home Court is "killing the court staff" because the increased workload can literally mean few if any breaks during the day. This type of regimen can be hard on judges, but it is brutal for court clerks who typically have hours of paper work to complete even after the judge leaves the bench.

Even judges and court personnel who do not handle domestic violence can be affected by the staffing of a specialized domestic violence court. Charlene Hiss, the District Court Administrator for Clark County in Vancouver, Washington, explained that it was difficult just to find a court-staffing schedule to which all the judges would agree. The Clark County District Court had a five-week criminal arraignment rotation for each of the five judges on the court. His attempted to schedule a four-week rotation schedule to allow Judge Fritzler to sit on the new domestic violence court. The other judges refused to accept the new schedule, and so Judge Fritzler is doing his share of the five-week rotation plus all of the domestic violence court.

Specialized domestic violence courts often mean the increased use of supervised probation for domestic violence offenders. Chuck Bristol, Court Services Supervisor for Clark Country District Court, noted that there had been over a 140% increase in supervised cases over the year and a half the domestic violence court had been in existence. There has been no increase in the probation staff to handle the additional work.

Specialized criminal domestic violence courts often mean additional court appearances to monitor the defendant's progress in batterer intervention programs. This may require the presence of prosecutors, defense attorneys and probation officers. The Sacramento Domestic Violence Home Court originally required offenders to appear in court to prove compliance with batterer intervention programs, but the time required for the court appearance and the extra paperwork that generated for the court clerks became unmanageable. The court is exploring the option of having probation officers ensure compliance so that court clerks do not have to handle the paperwork at the multiple court appearances.

4. High burnout- As Sacramento prosecutor Robert Morgester explained, "No judge wants to do Domestic Violence Home Court-more things can go wrong than can go right." Because of the high stakes involved in even misdemeanor domestic violence cases and the extreme workload, burnout is a very real problem for all court personnel.

Domestic violence cases are intensely emotional and can lead to great frustration for prosecutors, judges and probation officers. One prosecutor explained it as, "it's very hard to deal with individuals who don't want to help themselves." Prosecutors can lose sight of the fact that dealing with the criminal process is just a small piece of what the victim must cope with because of the violence in the victim's life. Domestic violence can lead to homelessness, unemployment, medical care and child care issues, all of which are beyond the expertise and duty of a prosecutor.

One way to deal with prosecutorial burnout is to limit victim contact by having witness assistants communicate with the victims. Dealing with a victim takes a lot of time and patience, and witness assistants are often trained counselors with (hopefully) expertise in assessing the level of lethality potential and connecting victims with appropriate resources.

Judith Shoshana, Director of the Seattle City Attorney's Domestic Violence Unit, noted that prosecutors on the specialized team tend to "max out" at two years. In Sacramento the average duration for prosecutors in the domestic violence unit is also two years. By extension, a fixed rotation period for judges, court clerks and probation officers should minimize the burn out factor. The period of rotation should allow the system to capitalize on the person's expertise gained through experience in the court for as long as possible while at the same time moving the person out of the specialized court before burnout affects the level of service.

# 4

# Domestic Violence

## DEFINITION OF DOMESTIC VIOLENCE

The federal legal definition of "domestic violence" differs from many state definitions, which may differ from the definition in a municipal ordinance. Some prosecutor's offices may restrict the definition for their domestic violence team to limit the number of cases a team has to handle, or it may expand the definition to ensure advocacy services for vulnerable victims. For example, many legal definitions of "domestic violence" include parties who have lived together, but many prosecutors' offices will give cases involving roommates with no romantic attachment to the regular trial team, not the domestic violence team. Prosecutors can also influence "domestic violence" dockets by not charging domestic assault and charging regular assault, trespass, robbery or some sort of other crime instead.

Child abuse and sexual abuse are often crimes prosecuted by attorneys in specialized units. Separating "child abuse" from "domestic violence" may obscure the reality of the family violence and cause duplicative or conflicting court orders (such as the child abuser who is also a domestic abuser being ordered by one court to take parenting classes in order to reunite with the child, while being ordered by another court to stay away from the child).

Courts may also limit the number of domestic violence cases by defining the definition of "domestic violence" more narrowly than the pertinent statute allows. The courts may follow the lead of the prosecutor's office in determining what cases are placed on the domestic violence calendar.

Any community considering a specialized criminal domestic violence court should consider whether the existing legal definition of a "domestic" relationship is too restrictive or expansive to be practical. The community must consider whether the definition of a "domestic" relationship should include:

1. Spouses and former spouses
2. Persons living together or have resided together in the past
3. Persons who have a child in common, including gay and lesbian parenting couples and cases where the woman is pregnant but the child has not been born
4. Persons related by blood or adoption, including parent-child, siblings, half-siblings and stepsiblings.
5. Gay and lesbian relationships
6. Persons involved in a significant sexual or romantic relationship

## BRINGING THE PLAYERS TO THE TABLE

Prosecutor Denice Biros of Vancouver, Washington noted that creation of a specialized domestic violence court is a "difficult process and what's really important is the cooperation of all the different agencies."

Judge Fritzler, the major force behind the creation of the Vancouver domestic violence court, explained that popular support, while essential, cannot sustain reform alone. It is a complicated process that can only be successful if all the essential participants and service providers are included in the process. All these participants must buy into the basic principles and concepts... [of a] dedicated domestic violence court.

Corrections Counselor Beth Sharpe of Clark County District Court noted the need in the planning process to "talk to rank and file people." She cautioned that it is "easy to make decisions at the top without understanding what will happen in day to day reality."

The challenge in beginning the process of creating a specialized domestic violence court is bringing together a group that includes the key players without it being too big to be unmanageable. The most important player is often the judiciary, because the court cannot specialize without the court itself deciding to do so.

Prior to 1998, the Clark County District Court in Vancouver, Washington had no specialization of any kind. Judge Fritzler envisioned a specialized domestic violence court with combined civil and criminal jurisdiction. With the help of a university professor to organize meetings for interested parties every two weeks for six months, Judge Fritzler had a domestic violence court up and running within a year and a half despite the reluctance of his fellow judges. Judge Fritzler described the purpose of the meetings as, "I wanted input, and I wanted everybody to have their say."

Any community considering creating a specialized criminal domestic violence court should consider ways to seek input from the following people:

- Judges
- Court Administrative personnel
- Court reporters
- Law clerks
- Prosecutors
- Misdemeanor
- Felony
- Federal
- Public Defenders
- Private criminal defense attorneys
- Police
- Sheriff
- Jail personnel

- Civil process servers
- Probation
- Treatment providers
- Government Officials
- City
- County
- State
- Federal
- Advocacy Community
- Survivors of Domestic Violence
- Communities of People of Color
- Non-English speaking communities
- Religious communities
- Gay and Lesbian communities
- Educational community
- Medical community

## FUNDING

The creation of the Sacramento Domestic Violence Home Court was made possible by a Violence Against Women Act (VAWA) grant in the amount of $939,020 in 1997. The Sacramento court applied for additional federal funding in 1998 of $2,100, 678 to continue the work of the court and provide for additional prosecutor, public defender, probation and court staff.

In contrast, the Clark Country Domestic Violence Court experience proved it was "possible to create a major innovative progressive court project within the existing structure of the court without extensive additional funding or outside sources of money." After the court was up and running the decision came to apply for a VAWA grant. The problem, according to Judge Fritzler, was that "everybody wanted a piece of it," including the sheriff's department, victim advocates of the YWCA, and treatment providers. Despite the difficulty of reaching consensus on the most pressing and necessary services needed, the grant request was submitted and is awaiting review.

Judge Fritzler stressed the importance of providing detailed "state of the court" reports to the county board to ensure consistent funding. Presentations by judges and court staff to the County Commissioners provided an important picture of the anticipated benefits of a specialized domestic violence court. The Superior Court has recently appropriated ten million dollars to construct a family court center that would provide increased security measures, child care, and meeting rooms for victims' advocates. Judge Fritzler fears that this appropriation is not enough to fund all the services desired.

## JURISDICTION

1. Civil and Criminal

The Clark County Domestic Violence Court hears both criminal misdemeanor domestic violence and petitions for Orders for Protection. This combined jurisdiction required the Superior Court to allow the District Court jurisdiction over the civil OFPs, matters previously heard only in Superior Court. Communities considering specialization should consider whether civil and criminal jurisdiction can and should be shared between two different court systems.

As discussed previously in this paper, combined jurisdiction may lead to increased pressure on the court and prosecutor to reduce or eliminate criminal consequences if the defendant cooperates in the divorce proceeding. In addition, combined jurisdiction may increase the possibility of a defendant's Fifth Amendment right being violated if s/he testifies at the civil proceedings, or it may increase the possibility of a victim being cross-examined by the criminal defense attorney.

The advantage of combined jurisdiction is that it reduces or eliminates the possibility of conflicting terms in OFPs and criminal "no contact" orders." As it is easier for the abuser to manipulate the court system when the abuser appears in front of multiple judges, combined jurisdiction may minimize this possibility.

2. Misdemeanor and felony

Many jurisdictions such as Seattle, Washington have separate courts and prosecuting authorities depending on whether the crime is a felony or misdemeanor. The Municipal Court of Seattle has a specialized domestic violence pretrial calendar for misdemeanor domestic violence cases, while felony domestic violence offenses are heard in Superior Court. The Seattle City Attorney's Domestic Violence Unit prosecutes misdemeanor cases. Court and prosecutor specialization occurs most often at the misdemeanor level because there are virtually always many more misdemeanor domestic violence cases in a jurisdiction than felony cases.

In contrast, the Domestic Violence Home Court for Sacramento County in California hears both misdemeanors and felonies, and the Domestic Violence Unit of the Sacramento District Attorney's Office prosecutes both levels of crime. Combining felony and misdemeanor jurisdiction may encourage both the court and the prosecutors to take all domestic violence seriously, rather than dismissing misdemeanor domestic violence as "just a misdemeanor." Effective intervention in domestic violence requires innovative approaches, and communities considering a specialized domestic violence court might consider the possibility of combining court and prosecutorial jurisdiction for misdemeanor and felony crimes.

The biggest roadblock to combining jurisdiction is that it may take an actual change in the state law to allow it to happen. Both courts and prosecutor's offices guard their jurisdictions jealously, and any attempt to combine jurisdiction may be perceived as a loss of power and/or an undesired increase in workload. Some prosecutor's offices aggressively prosecute domestic violence while others may not; combining jurisdiction in one office may simply lead to less aggressive prosecution.

3. Selecting Judges and Prosecutors

a. Judge acceptable to prosecution and defense

Because both prosecutors and defense attorneys can remove a judge without a stated reason once in a criminal proceeding, it is important that any judge on a domestic violence court be acceptable to both sides. Otherwise, one side could routinely file an affidavit of prejudice on the judge, disrupting the smooth operation of the court. Another option is to have a designated second (or even third) judge; thus, if one side filed on the judge, all parties would know who the alternate judge would be.

b. Prosecutors

All three prosecutor offices in the jurisdictions surveyed for this paper took volunteers for their specialized domestic violence units. This helps ensure that the units self-select prosecutors that have some degree of victim sensitivity.

The Sacramento District Attorney's Office requires a prosecutor to have some experience in a "victim-sensitive" area (sex crimes or domestic violence) to be eligible for promotion to the highest attorney level. This helps ensure that the prosecutors in these units receive some professional status and that sex crimes and domestic violence are not just dismissed as "women's issues." On the other hand, this promotional requirement may mean that prosecutors will request the sex crimes and domestic violence units simply to fulfill the requirement. These prosecutors may not have a high degree of understanding of the complex dynamics of family violence, or the desire to learn those dynamics.

It is worth noting that prior to the creation of the new Domestic Violence Unit in Sacramento, all the attorneys handling domestic violence cases in the old Domestic Violence Unit were women. Now the supervisor and two lead attorneys are male, as are approximately half of the other attorneys in the unit (the current District Attorney is a woman). The influx of money, resources, status and promotional opportunities into a specialized prosecutor unit or court may affect the gender balance in the unit.

## EXPERIENCE

As a general estimate, one prosecutor stated that 80% of victims recant or minimize the assault at some point in the criminal justice process. Often, prosecutors will dismiss a case upon the recantation of a victim. In the Sacramento District Attorney's Domestic Violence Unit, prosecutors must have tried over ten jury trials before coming to the unit. The theory is that experienced trial attorneys are better able to try a case without a victim. Before the Domestic Violence Unit and Domestic Violence Home Court, the average number of domestic violence trials was twenty-one per year. In 1997 there was only one misdemeanor domestic violence jury trial. In 1998 the Domestic Violence Unit tried over thirty jury trials, including ten misdemeanor cases and four cases without a victim.

## PHYSICAL FACILITIES

Domestic violence cases involve not only increased personnel such as probation officers and witness assistants and/or victim advocates, but defendants and victims often have children, family and friends accompany them to court. This requires a courtroom with adequate space. Increased courtroom security is necessary to ensure that victims are not contacted by the defendant in the courtroom as well as walking to and from the courtroom. Ideally, the court provides a separate waiting area for victims. Finally, the large number of defendants typically in custody may require a large holding facility in the courtroom, as well as additional jailers to move the defendant to and from court.

## PROBATION

Court services (probation) officers may perform a variety of functions, including making a lethality assessment for the case, making victim contact by phone or in court, and providing recommendations for release and sentencing conditions. Both the Vancouver, Washington and the Sacramento, California Domestic Violence Courts require automatic court appearances by defendants to check on the status of their participation in batterer intervention programs. Out of court, probation officers may be required to monitor defendants on supervised or intensive probation, meeting with the defendant on weekly or monthly schedules to monitor progress.

## OPPOSITION TO SPECIALIZED COURT

1. Judicial opposition

Judges may be opposed to the creation of a specialized criminal domestic violence courts. Judge Randal Fritzler of the Clark County Domestic Violence Court explained: Elected judges seem to believe they have a mandate from the people and a right to conduct their court as if it were their own little kingdom. This individualistic predisposition, when combined with the desire to protect and maintain their own self-contained courtroom, creates resistance to change. Many judges also fear that any change which expands the duties of judges will substantially increase their workload. These factors, together with everything else which normally create resistance to change (including jealousy, fear of the unknown and concern that another judge may obtain some political advantage) make it perilous to embark upon a major court project.

Typically, chief judges may have the authority to handle administrative decisions for the court, but not to supervise or order other judges to do things. Major decisions such as adopting and implementing a specialized court system require the majority approval of the other judges even if the chief judge supports the project. When judges are resistant to change, the best incentive may be positive publicity by external agencies such as victim advocacy groups for judges who focus on and support court improvements for domestic violence.

2. Opposition by Criminal Defense Bar

Criminal defense attorneys may perceive a specialized criminal domestic violence court as biased against defendants and therefore may work against the creation of such a court. Defendants may file an affidavit of prejudice on a judge, meaning that the defendant may exercise his/her right to remove a judge without a stated reason once during the course of a criminal proceeding. Defense attorneys will advise their clients to exercise this right if the defense attorney perceives bias on the part of the judge. If defendants filed routinely on the judges in a specialized domestic violence court, it would seriously impair the smooth operation of the court. Thus, the defense bar has a strong bargaining chip in the operation of any criminal court.

One way to counter the perception of bias in a specialized criminal domestic violence court is to include public defenders and members of the private criminal defense bar in the creation of the specialized court from the beginning. Although public defenders were "reluctant" to assist in the creation of the Clark County Domestic Violence Court, it did give them an opportunity to voice any misgivings about the court's creation and operation. To date, the defense attorneys in all three courts surveyed in this paper have not abused the right to remove the judge.

3. Opposition by Prosecutors

Opposition by prosecutors may not appear as outright hostility because no prosecutor wants to look "soft" on domestic violence. Instead, prosecutorial opposition to a specialized domestic violence court may surface in the adoption of office policies at odds with the goals of a specialized court. For example, while the Clark County Domestic Violence Court was being created, the "prosecuting attorney's office selected late 1997 to revive its previously abandoned 'domestic violence diversion program.'" The problem with the diversion program was that it sent the message that some domestic violence is not serious, reduced certainty of punishment for batterers, and removed a significant number of cases from the criminal process. It is important to uncover prosecutorial opposition early in the process so that there can be complete buy-in by the prosecutor in the specialized domestic violence court.

4. Opposition by Communities of Color

Depending on the composition and history of the community, any "get tough" policy on the part of the criminal justice system can be perceived to unfairly target communities of color. Specialization of criminal domestic violence courts may be viewed as part of a "get tough" movement. It is important that community dialogue not pit fairness to men of color against the safety of women; both values can be served by a specialized criminal domestic violence court that provides accessibility to the victim and attention to the constitutional rights of the defendant.

## MEASUREMENT OF OUTCOME

Any community considering the specialization of a criminal domestic violence court must determine what a "successful" court would look like and how a "successful" court would be measured. Speedy disposition of cases, judges able to make decisions based on law specific to domestic violence cases, consistency of sentencing, victim satisfaction with court experience, escalating punishment for escalating violence and reduced recidivism are all possible desired outcomes.

The Sacramento Domestic Violence Home Court is seeking to measure outcomes by having probation officers use an automated data collection form from the California State Department of Public Health to track defendant completion of batterer intervention programs. Public Health departments and local colleges and universities are good places for a court to seek help with the measurement of outcomes and project evaluations.

## CONCLUSION

As Judge Fritzler of the Clark County District Court stated, "there's no silver bullet to solve [the] problem" of domestic violence. The Clark County Domestic Violence Court was up and running in one and a half years; the fact that this is possible does not mean it is always desirable. Specialized criminal domestic violence courts are one possible step for a community to take, but there should not be a rush to judgment. Every community must weigh its own history, resources and desired outcome to determine if a specialized criminal domestic violence court is appropriate. In the end, it may be the dialogue to consider the possibility of a special court that might prove to be the most valuable tool of all, as each part of the community seeks to articulate a shared vision of justice.

## REVIEWING DOMESTIC VIOLENCE FATALITIES

## INTRODUCTION

This document brings together information from across the country on domestic violence fatality reviews. The document:

- Defines domestic violence;
- Provides a state-by-state matrix of domestic violence death review initiatives;
- Introduces teams' philosophies and some overarching philosophical questions;
- Introduces a selection of the purposes and goals of teams;
- Addresses team membership;
- Explores death review team protocols;
- Confronts concerns regarding confidentiality, liability, and immunity;
- Offers a selection of questions, issues, concerns, and investigative methods already used by teams as they conduct death reviews;
- Talks about the issue of effecting change through the process of reviewing domestic fatalities.

The full appendices listed in the print (not online) version offer an overview of existing research into domestic homicide and provide a variety of sample documents from selected states and jurisdictions who are at various stages in implementing fatality reviews. Many of these forms were not available in an electronic format and are therefore not available online at this time.

## WORKING DEFINITIONS

*Statutory definitions of domestic violence vary from state to state. For the purposes of this document, "domestic violence fatalities" refer to those homicides caused by domestic violence. The National*

*Council of Juvenile and Family Court Judges'* Model Code on Domestic and Family Violence *defines domestic violence as one or more of the below acts:*

i. Attempting to cause or causing physical harm to another family member or household member;

ii. Placing a family or household member in fear of physical harm; or

iii. Causing a family or household member to engage involuntarily in sexual activity by force, threat of force, or duress.

Preventable Death: "A preventable death is one in which, with retrospective analysis, it is determined that a reasonable intervention, (e.g., medical, educational, social, legal, psychological) might have prevented the death" (Colorado Child Fatality Review Commission Annual Report and Conference Proceedings, p. 15, 1991).

Reasonable: is defined by "taking into consideration the condition, circumstances or resources available" (Colorado Child Fatality Review Commission Annual Report and Conference Proceedings, p. 15, 1991).

Domestic violence death review: "means the deliberative process for identification of deaths, both homicide and suicide, caused by domestic violence, for examination of the systemic interventions into known incidents of domestic violence occurring in the family of the deceased prior to the death, for consideration of altered systemic response to avert future domestic violence deaths, or for development of recommendations for coordinated community prevention and intervention initiatives to eradicate, domestic violence."

## STATE-BY-STATE MATRIX OF DOMESTIC VIOLENCE DEATH REVIEW INITIATIVES

The following is a synopsis of known domestic violence fatality review activity on a state-by-state basis.

For each state the synopsis includes a discussion of legislation introduced; the names and contact information for known fatality review teams, or committees constituted to work toward the formation of such teams; the specific foci of teams; and, examples of reviews conducted by teams or other bodies.

i. California

California Penal Code s 11163.3 (a) provides for the establishment of county-level interagency domestic violence death review teams. These teams investigate both homicides and suicides related to domestic violence. The teams serve to ensure the role of domestic violence is recognized and that subsequent preventive measures are introduced.

California Penal Code s 11163.5 provides for the coordination and integration of state and local efforts to address fatal domestic violence and creates a body of information, the use of which is designed to prevent domestic violence deaths. The legislation charges the California Department of Justice with the task of carrying out reviews. The California Department of Justice is to proceed with the cooperation of the state Department of Social Services, the state Department of Health Services, the California State Coroner's Association, the county Welfare Director's Association, and the state domestic violence coalition. The Department of Justice produces an annual report of domestic violence deaths. Local teams report findings to the Department of Justice. Area agencies participating in the death reviews will finance the contributions of their team members. The state will not bear the costs of local teams.

ii. Los Angeles County's Team Stated Goals

The Los Angeles County (California) Domestic Violence Fatality Review Team, formed in 1993 under the Chairship of Alana Bowman, identified four primary goals:

i. Establish the means to determine with accuracy the number of homicides and suicides related to domestic violence;
ii. Identify resources for appropriate on-site counseling services at the scene of a homicide or suicide;

iii. Analyze patterns common to abusers and victims for possible identification as lethality assessment indicators;

iv. Develop systematic analysis of selected cases, focusing on the flow of each case through the various agencies in the system for indications of areas of improvement of strengthening of agency contacts and interagency response.

iii. The Charan Investigation

This domestic violence fatality review, conducted by the Commission on the Status of Women, City and County of San Francisco, is one of the most detailed ever conducted of a particular case. The Charan Investigation took place before the California legislation on domestic violence fatality reviews was introduced. Joseph Charan murdered his wife, Veena Charan, on January 15, 1990, and then took his own life. Veena Charan had sought the support of various government agencies for a period of 15 months prior to her demise. Veena had been separated from Joseph and was awarded custody of their nine-year-old son.

During the 15 months preceding her death she made numerous reports to the police. Immediately prior to her death Joseph was arrested for felony wife beating and malicious mischief. As a result of his conviction for this offense Joseph received a 12-month suspended jail sentence. He was put on probation through the Adult Probation Department with the following three conditions: 1. domestic violence counseling; 2. stay away order; and 3. 30 days jail, of which he was given four days, the remainder to be served in the Sheriff's Work Alternative Program. Veena Charan obtained a restraining order through the civil courts. Mr. Charan violated the restraining order on several occasions. He also attempted to kidnap his son at the son's school. It was at the school that Mr. Charan killed his wife in front of school teachers and school children, before committing suicide.

The San Francisco Domestic Violence Consortium which commissioned the Charan investigation requested answers to three clusters of questions:

1. Do the departments of the City and County of San Francisco have policies and procedures relating to domestic violence? If so, what are they and how adequate are they?
2. Is there sufficient information-sharing among the departments in these particular types of cases?
3. Are there sufficient data to evaluate the effectiveness of the system? If not, what additional data need to be collected? What changes, if any, to current procedures can be adopted to avert future tragedies?

The case files and public testimony identified four essential gaps in service delivery in the Charan case:

1. Communication and Coordination- Aside from the communication between the San Francisco Police Department and the District Attorney's Office, there was little communication among the multiple agencies which had contact with Veena Charan. These multiple agencies included the municipal court, adult probation, family court services, and social services. The review committee called for centralization of information and better coordination of service delivery.
2. Data Collection- The commission recognized the need for systematic information about domestic violence cases. The investigation notes, "Data on the number of domestic violence cases handled by the departments ranged from very limited to none at all." The Commission deemed the data to be of central importance in the identification of the level of need for services and the subsequent delivery of those services.
3. Access to Services- The Commission pointed out that a lack of sensitivity to and an understanding of multicultural and gay/lesbian issues in city departments increases the numbers of those suffering from domestic violence.
4. Training- Most of the training recommendations pertained to the issues regarding multicultural awareness. Translation services were lacking. Specifically, there was

a lack of translators in the Superior Court, Civil Division, and a limited number of translators in the Criminal Division. This problem created delays and misunderstandings of the agreements/court orders and proceedings. Specifically, the investigation called for the development of domestic violence advisory committees in each city department that worked with domestic violence cases.

Other excerpts from the Charan Investigation noted:

- Based on the incident reports involving Joseph Charan, the San Francisco Police Department did not deem the injuries Veena Charan and other family members received at the hands of Joseph Charan to be serious. Specifically, the report finds that "had the investigator looked at the pattern of violence established by Mr. Charan, and presented that information to the District Attorney's Office, stronger measures and responses to the situation may have prevented Joseph Charan from continuing the escalation of violence that led to the murder-suicide."
- According to the felony protocol of the District Attorney's Office, prior history was one of the factors taken into account regarding re-booking. If the Assistant District Attorney had access to the same information the Commission did, the re-booking charges may have been different.
- Probation officers were not adequately trained in the dynamics of domestic violence.
- The Commission called for greater domestic violence training of the Municipal Court, Criminal Division. In particular, it stated a "need for training judges on interpretation of restraining orders."
- Family Court Services refused to answer questions posed by the Commission, citing their need to maintain confidentiality. The Commission described this failure as "intransigence." The report states the resistance of Family Court Services "is indicative of the lack of the department's efforts to improve the City's response to

battered women and their children." The mediation strategies of the Family Court were also criticized by the Commission.

Final Report: Santa Clara County (California) Death Review Committee, October 1997

The Committee began work in 1994 and appears to have been among the first domestic violence review teams in the country. It defined "domestic violence related death" as one where the perpetrator and victim were "romantically linked," either at the time of death or prior to the death. At time of writing the Committee is reviewing 51 cases. Members selected three cases from 1993 to get started. The report contains information on:

- The types of deaths: homicide, homicide-suicide, suicide, accidental death, and police shootings.
- The police agencies involved in the case. Most involved the San Jose police department.
- The age, race, sex, and substance abuse history of any parties; the presence of children; weaponry used; status of the relationship (divorced, cohabiting, separated, etc.); existence of prior restraining orders; prior police involvement; and location of residence.

Highlights of the final report include:

- Age: average adult age of perpetrators and victims was 33 years (females 32; males 35).
- Sex of perpetrators: 44 male, seven female.
- 29 of the 51 homicides were committed with firearms. The report stresses that "as a community we must advocate for handgun control."
- In 26 of the 51 cases the parties were separated or divorced at time of death.
- Police had prior domestic violence contacts with the parties in 11 cases.
- In six cases restraining orders were either active (four) or in the process of being issued (two).
- Race/Ethnicity: of the 51 victims, 17 were Asian, 14 white,

12 Hispanic, five African American, two mixed-races, one Indian (not Native American). Asian victims were over-represented among victims although only one of the Asian cases came to the attention of community agencies prior to the killing. The report notes, "This made members feel that we were not getting the word out about the dangers of domestic violence to the Asian community." This led to calls for greater Asian representation on the death review committee. The report notes three Asian members on the team. One committee member helped form the Asian Community Against Domestic Violence Coalition. This Coalition organized a domestic violence conference for the Vietnamese community in September 1997.

The suggestion that more Asian women need to be accessed through support services should not be taken to mean that those women who do not utilize services are somehow culpable for their own deaths. Karin Wang (1996) points to the way the cultural background of Asian women makes it difficult for them to utilize the support services offered by a predominantly white-run domestic violence movement. In addressing this issue, Wang argues that battered Asian-American women have not been well understood by the domestic violence movement.

- The California legislation does not address the issue of domestic violence shelters turning over their records for purposes of death review. The reason offered in the report is that shelters were concerned about sharing information given by clients under guarantee of confidentiality. Informally, the team seems to have worked around this issue and it appears that a mechanism has emerged so that shelter team members do share information.
- The report also contains a list of questions that the team sought to answer regarding the delivery of services to families prior to the killing.

iv. Delaware

Delaware Statute Title 13 s 2105 empowers a domestic violence coordinating council to investigate and review, through a review panel, the facts and circumstances of all deaths occurring in Delaware resulting from domestic violence. This includes homicides and suicides. Reviews of deaths involving criminal investigations will be delayed at least six months from the time of death and must be authorized by the Attorney General's office. Child deaths are to be reviewed jointly by the Child Death Review Commission and the domestic violence fatal incident review panel. The death of a minor will be reviewed by the domestic violence fatal incident review panel only if the child's parents or guardians were involved in an abusive relationship and where the minor's death is directly related to that abuse.

i. District of Columbia

Charlotte Clark U.S. District Attorney's Office Judiciary Center, Room 3433 Washington DC 20001 202-514-7375

The committee has plans to review cases from 1992 up to the present time, but only after the resolution of any pending criminal charges. They have suspended their meetings until they are able to obtain more funding.

ii. Florida

The Florida Department of Law Enforcement reported 230 domestic homicides for 1994. As a result of this disturbing statistic the Florida Governor's Task Force on Domestic and Sexual Violence funded a study of domestic fatalities in order to better understand, intervene, and prevent these crimes.

## METHODOLOGY

For each domestic fatality in 1994 the researchers examined the following:

- The perpetrator-victim dyad: In particular the researchers examined the multiple dynamics of these murders, paying particular attention to the sex, race, ethnicity, sexual orientation, geo-cultural background (rural, suburban, urban), socioeconomic status, and marital status/familial relationship between perpetrators and victims.
- The situational antecedents to the fatality: Researchers

explored the following:

1. A prior history of domestic violence in the relationship.
2. The presence or absence of injunctions both prior to the fatality or when the fatality occurred.
3. Whether a divorce was pending at the time of death (with married couples).
4. Whether there was any sign of relationship breakdown (variously measured).
5. Whether there was any sign of acknowledged conflict in the relationship.
6. Prior police calls to residence.
7. History of drug/alcohol abuse.
8. The residential origins of the perpetrator and victim. Was there a pattern of perpetrators abducting or transporting victims to areas beyond their regular communities before the fatality?
9. Whether the victim or perpetrator had any history of emotional problems or mental illness and the specific forms of these problems. Had the perpetrator:

- Previously threatened to kill himself, his spouse, partner, or children?
- Fantasized, hatched a plan, or verbalized a plan to kill his spouse/partner?
- A history of using weapons, especially firearms?
- Obsessively possessive beliefs about his spouse or partner?
- Perceived his spouse/partner was betraying him by ending the relationship?
- Been hospitalized for depression and fantasized about killing his partner?
- A history of hostage-taking
- The lethal incident: Here researchers documented:
    1. The specific mode of killing.
    2. The types of weaponry used (handgun, rifle, shotgun, other firearm, knife or cutting instrument, blunt object, motor vehicle, poison, explosives, fire or incendiary device, personal weapons such as fists, feet, teeth, etc.).

3. The availability of weapons.
4. The involvement of drugs or alcohol during or immediately preceding the fatal episode.
5. The presence of other parties at the scene (e.g. children, police, other professionals).
6. The non-fatal wounding of others at the scene.
7. The involvement of professionals at the scene.
8. The location of the fatal incident.

Researchers drew information from the following data sources: police records; social service reports; court documents; newspaper accounts; autopsy reports; mental health records; hospital and public health/medical data; and, other information that may have had a bearing on the decedent and their family. They also interviewed professionals including but not limited to police, court personnel, mental health workers, social service providers, and advocates for battered women.

## KEY FINDINGS

The Florida Department of Law Enforcement (FDLE) documented 230 domestic fatalities in Florida during the year of 1994. Perhaps the most important and compelling finding in this study was that the research revealed a total of 328 domestic fatalities in 1994. The disparity stemmed from four major issues:

1. Police departments often do not include child deaths due to abuse and neglect as part of their official domestic homicide count. The researchers included these deaths.
2. Police departments often do not include the suicide victims in domestic homicide-suicides in their official count. The researchers included these deaths. However, the researchers did not include those deaths from suicide that are related to domestic violence. This figure, largely unknown at this time, represents a huge number of potential deaths stemming from domestic victimization and is an area in urgent need of systematic research and policy initiatives.

3. Police sometimes did not code domestic deaths as such.
4. Police departments did not include boyfriend/girlfriend deaths as domestic homicides because they did not strictly meet the terms of the statute.

Adopting a broader definition of domestic homicide than law enforcement sources, the researchers showed that in 1994 approximately one-third of all homicides were related to domestic violence. This ratio contrasts sharply with official police data which identifies only one-fifth of all homicides in Florida in 1994 as being caused by domestic violence. The essential findings from the 1994 Florida report on domestic violence deaths are shown below.

The analysis indicated that 294 of the 328 fatalities were consistent with the Florida Domestic Violence Statute. The 34 remaining domestic fatalities either fell outside the statute criteria (e.g. victim and perpetrator were not married, lived at different addresses, and had no children together) or the researchers simply did not have enough information to determine if they met all the criteria of the statute.

Nearly all cases with multiple victims were perpetrated by men. In only six cases did a woman kill more than one victim, or murder her partner and then commit suicide. In no case did a woman murder her husband, her children, and then herself.

Many of the factors present in the multiple domestic killings also appear in the killing of individual women. Most of the individual women were killed by men. Nearly all of these cases involved women who had an extensive history of violent victimization prior to being killed. As the statistical analysis reveals, other important factors include prior threats to kill, escalating abuse, and obsessive possessiveness and jealousy on the part of perpetrators. In fewer cases there was prior documented involvement of police and other criminal justice agencies. Of all adult women victims, only three were killed by other women. Five adult female fatalities resulted from women killing themselves as part of multiple killing scenarios.

When women are killed in either multiple or single-victim domestic fatalities, it is usually the final event in an abusive relationship of long standing. When men are killed by other men or by women, it is rarely, if ever, the end-product of a battering relationship in which the men are the victims of abuse. When men are killed by other men in domestic situations, it is often because the two men are competing for a woman who has, in many cases, been victimized by one of the men. Three-quarters of all adult male domestic fatalities were perpetrated by men. Only one-quarter of the men who died were killed by women.

Women who killed men nearly always did so out of self-defense, or less often, the defense of their children. These women have always, or nearly always, been pushed to the brink of human endurance by the batterers who they eventually kill. While the killing of batterers by the long-standing victims of battering may not qualify as self-defense in a court of law, the act of defensive or preemptive violence by women is qualitatively different from the offensive acts of violence perpetrated by men against women.

The statistical analysis of child fatalities is hampered by missing data. Nevertheless, there are certain themes that seem to pervade these tragedies. The most common correlate is that the death of children resulting from abuse or neglect, occurs in homes where caretakers tend not to be married. About one-third of the perpetrators were mother's boyfriends, one-third were biological fathers, and approximately a quarter were biological mothers. These men sometimes had criminal records, including a history of violence. It is clear from multiple sources of data that child fatalities normally occur within a context of poverty, often abject poverty. Research findings also reveal that 50 percent of the children about whom we have reliable data have been physically abused before, often for a long period of time. However, it is not necessarily the case that this prior abuse has come to the attention of authorities. For example, very few of the families in which child fatalities occurred had prior documented contact with the police. Children who are under five years of age are clearly the most vulnerable. Over half of the child victims in our sample were under two years of age. Those who were older were often killed with easily obtained firearms.

"Red Flags" (situational antecedents) identified in order of frequency in the 106 cases where men killed in intimate female partners in Florida in 1994.

1. Prior history of domestic violence. Among these cases battered women often report an increasing entrapment.
2. Obsessively possessive beliefs on the part of the perpetrator. This is often accompanied by stalking behavior, close surveillance, inability to sleep on the part of the perpetrator, acute depression, perhaps a history of medication use, history of suicidal ideations, or, less commonly, documented suicide attempts.
3. Attempting to break away from the perpetrator, including divorce, separation, and estrangement. In a number of cases of breaking away researchers identified accompanying relationship difficulties regarding such matters as child custody/visitation.
4. Prior police involvement in the case.
5. Prior criminal history on the part of the perpetrator. In 43 percent of those cases where men killed their intimate female partners in non-multiple episodes, the men had prior histories of criminal behavior, nearly always involving violence.
6. Threats to kill the eventual victim. These were often communicated to family friends, relatives, neighbors, and others prior to the homicide.
7. Issuance of restraining orders (injunctions, protection orders).
8. Alcohol or drug use that often escalates prior to the fatal episode.

i. Iowa

Probation Officer Tracy Bray and the Iowa Coalition Against Domestic Violence initiated the Iowa Domestic Violence Fatality Review Team project, which has yet to review a domestic fatality. Law enforcement had concerns about being a target or scapegoat, but once they were on board many others followed; their legislation passed in the 1998 session. The Iowa Department of Public Health is the administrative agency and they are absorbing all additional expenses for the project. They anticipate reviewing approximately 12 domestic violence fatalities a year.

ii. Kentucky

No legislation passed and no teams are in place as yet. However, the attorney general's office did conduct a synopsis of patterns of domestic violence related deaths.

Kentucky Attorney General's Task Force on Domestic Violence Crime: Domestic Violence Homicides and Suicides, October 1993.

This report emerged out of a broad initiative in Kentucky to increase awareness of domestic violence, a concern to furnish women and families with better state services, and a need to standardize data collection on domestic violence in general and domestic violence homicides and suicides in particular. The report summarizes the findings on domestic violence homicides and suicides which occurred in 1991, 1992, and the first quarter of 1993. The specific goals of the report were to collect and analyze all available data on domestic violence related homicides and suicides for the following purposes:

- To increase public and professional awareness about these particular crimes, the persons involved, and intervention measures utilized to prevent the homicide and suicide incidents.
- To improve the effectiveness of justice and community services planning for intervention in and prevention of these crimes.
- To improve the collection and reporting of domestic violence homicide and suicide incidents at the local, state, and national levels. The preliminary findings revealed:
- 77 domestic violence related homicide and suicide incidents for 1991 (resulting in 95 deaths).

- 63 incidents in 1992 (resulting in 74 deaths).
- 23 incidents in the first quarter of 1993 (resulting in 30 deaths).
- For the whole period, 96 male perpetrators killed 23 men and 82 women.
- For the whole period, 48 female perpetrators killed 48 men and no women.
- Domestic violence related homicides constituted 27 percent of all Kentucky homicides in 1991 and 22 percent of homicides in 1992.
- Firearms were used to effect the majority of homicides (73 percent in 1991; 69 percent in 1992; 64 percent for the first quarter 1993).

iii. Maine

The Maine Commission on Domestic Abuse was constituted under Title 5, section 12004-I, subsection 74-C., and was required to establish the Domestic Abuse Homicide Review Panel, referred to in this subsection as the "panel," to review the deaths of persons who are killed by family or household members as defined by section 4002.

A. According to the legislation, the chair of the commission shall appoint members of the panel who have experience in providing services to victims of domestic abuse and shall include at least the following: the Chief Medical Examiner, a physician, a nurse, a law enforcement officer, the Commissioner of Human Services, the Commissioner of Corrections, the Commissioner of Public Safety, a judge as assigned by the Chief Justice of the Supreme Judicial Court, a representative of the Maine Prosecutor's Association, an assistant attorney general responsible for the prosecution of homicide cases designated by the Attorney General, an assistant attorney general handling child protection cases designated by the Attorney General, a victim-witness advocate, a mental health service provider, a facilitator of a certified batterers' intervention program under section 4014 and three persons designated by a statewide coalition for family crisis services.

B. The panel shall recommend to state and local agencies methods of improving the system for protecting persons from domestic abuse, including modifications of laws, rules, policies, and procedures following completion of adjudication.

C. The panel shall collect and compile data related to domestic abuse.

iv. New Mexico

The University of New Mexico Department of Emergency Medicine is the administrative agency for their local domestic violence fatality review team. They initiated their effort in July, 1997 with a one-year Violence Against Women Act grant. All team members must sign a confidentiality agreement to enable them to share confidential information. With the exception of medical records, they have encountered little resistance to acquiring information when it is available. They are not pursuing legislation at this time. New Mexico had approximately 45-50 domestic violence fatalities in 1997.

v. New York

Bob Nicholais Staff Member on Commission New York State Office for the Prevention of Domestic Violence Capital View Office Park 52 Washington Street, Room 366 Rensselaer, New York 12144 518-486-6262.

The Governor established a commission for a one-year review of domestic violence related homicides. A report of these findings entitled the "Commission on Domestic Violence Fatalities: Report to the Governor 1997" became available in October 1997. The Commission is still active with one full-time and one part-time paid position. New York City also produced a report on female homicides entitled, "Female Homicide Victims in New York City 1990-1994" available from: NYC Dept. of Health, Injury Prevention Program, 2 Lafayette Street, 20th Floor, New York, New York 10007.

## EXISTING REVIEWS

Commission on Domestic Violence Fatalities: Report to the Governor, 1997.

The Commission was appointed by Executive Order of Governor George Pataki on October 1, 1996. It was charged with the responsibility to "investigate select domestic violence fatalities to determine whether the deaths were associated with any deficiencies in the social service system, law enforcement, the courts, or any other public or private entity." One of the tasks of the commission was to "assess whether a Fatality Review Board should be created to examine domestic violence fatalities." The commission was appointed in response to a number of high-profile domestic homicides that occurred when other forms of violent crime (e.g. murder, robbery, aggravated assault) in New York were declining.

Highlights of the 57 deaths, reviewed by the Commission include:

- In most of the cases domestic violence preceded the homicide. In 70 percent of cases the perpetrator had a known history of physically abusing the decedent. Only six cases (11 percent) revealed no known history of prior abuse.
- Twenty-six of the 57 perpetrators (45.6 percent) had a prior criminal record of one or more arrests. All but four of those 26 offenders had prior arrests for domestic violence.
- In 21 of the 57 cases (36.8 percent) there was at least one active order of protection. In 17 of these 21 cases (81 percent) there had been a violation of an order prior to the homicide.
- Forty-three of the 57 victims (75 percent) had terminated, or had indicated an intention to terminate, their relationships at the time of the homicide.
- Reviewers found child custody disputes at the roct of three homicides. In two of these three cases the homicide was committed in connection with the pick-up or drop-off of children.
- Most homicides took place in the home (75 percent). Nine percent occurred in the workplace and 11 percent in other public areas.

- Handguns were used in 20 (35 percent) of the cases; long guns in nine (16 percent). Of the 20 handguns used only four were possessed lawfully.
- Of the 57 offenders, 27 (47 percent) had indications of a history of alcohol abuse and 17 (30 percent) had indications of a history of drug use. These 44 offenders with a history of substance abuse included 12 with a history of both alcohol and drug use.
- The Commission makes the point that in 30 percent of cases there was no known history of domestic violence in the relationship. They conclude that the absence of any reported violence should not lead to the conclusion that there is a low-risk of mortality.
- Disappointingly, the Commission did not recommend the establishment of domestic fatality review teams.

## EXISTING REVIEWS

### The Deliberations of the Philadelphia Team

The Philadelphia Team makes the following important observations about the deaths of women:

1. It is difficult to locate information on many of the female decedents, especially psycho-social data. Many of these women led invisible lives and their deaths often went unnoticed. Many of the women who die prematurely are not known to any community/legal systems.
2. Perpetrators of domestic homicide are often known within their communities and not only in their role as offenders. Some are known to mental health providers. The team asks whether it is not possible to flag or track such offenders who need but refuse psychiatric help.
3. Gun merchants do not always refuse to sell firearms to individuals with Protection from Abuse Orders against them. Additionally, judges do not always order perpetrators in domestic violence situations to relinquish previously acquired weapons. The team raises a number of questions about the use of the judiciary to remove or manage access to weaponry.

4. Women who die from HIV/AIDS are often connected to lifestyles involving drug use and prostitution. It is well documented that prostitutes suffer inordinate amounts of abuse at the hands of men. Indeed there is a clear correlation between women enduring lives as prostitutes and women's poverty and interpersonal brutalization. There is also a growing literature pointing to the vulnerability of battered women to HIV infections.

vi. Tennessee

According to Tennessee's pending legislation they will have a state panel attached to the Department of Health. Some of the duties of the state panel will include: reviewing reports from local domestic violence lethality and fatality review panels; making recommendations for any changes to laws, rules, and policies that would promote the safety and well-being of families and children of domestic violence; undertaking annual statistical studies of the incidence and cause of domestic violence fatalities; providing training and written materials to the local panels; developing protocols for the collection of data; providing technical assistance to local panels; and periodically assessing the operations of domestic violence lethality and fatality prevention efforts.

They are to establish a minimum of one local panel in each judicial district. The local panels are to: review all deaths related to domestic violence; collect and submit data to the state panel; submit recommendations and advocate for system improvements and resources where gaps and deficiencies may exist; and participate in training provided by the state panel.

vii. West Virginia

The Supreme Court of Appeals voted unanimously to establish fatality review teams in December, 1994. The role of the fatality review teams is to examine court cases where a death has occurred in order to identify any patterns or trends that may be present, to examine court procedures to determine whether proper steps were taken, to review applicable statutes and rules to see whether amendments are needed, and to assess whether other involved agencies followed required processes and whether there was a coordinated effort among agencies to address the issues in the case.

The West Virginia program does not focus on domestic violence deaths only, although they do acknowledge most of the cases reviewed are domestic violence related. In 1997 they reviewed four cases involving five deaths. One was a murder-suicide. The administrative director of the program reviews cases to determine if they meet their criteria. Then the case is shown to the Chief Justice of the State Supreme Court, if they concur the case is referred to one of their three Fatality Review Teams. A case is never reviewed by the team from the community in which the death occurred. The team will examine the case, produce findings, and develop recommendations. This information is given to the Chief Justice of the State Supreme Court who may make recommendations to the Supreme Court. This document is not public; however, a synopsis of all the fatality review team reports is produced each calendar year.

## FATALITY REVIEW TEAM PHILOSOPHIES

Domestic violence fatality review committees have learned much from death reviews in the field of medicine. The medical review model is based on the internal reviews of deaths that occur in hospital settings. Personnel involved with patients who die in questionable circumstances present information to the team. The team gathers the information together and reaches a conclusion about the reasons for the fatality. Teams adopting the medical review model should be aware of one of the earlier problems in this process, namely, "catching rascals, rather than on improving hospital wide performance" (Rosen and Susman, 1983). Child fatality review teams initially emerged with a punitive ethos. In particular, some teams sought to identify breakdowns in the system of service delivery. Later teams focused less on individual accountability and more on system-wide service coordination. However, as the Colorado Committee points out, if cases are handled improperly, or if a crime is committed, agencies with the greatest involvement and clearest responsibility are asked to put things right. In especially egregious situations, matters can be submitted to a grand jury.

Domestic violence fatality reviews that have gotten off the ground in a small number of states have tried to adhere to this no-blame and shame ethos. Examples where this philosophy is explicitly written into the operational protocols include the reviews in Hawaii conducted out of Judge Michael Town's office and the Project Safeguard reviews through the City of Denver. For example, the mission statement of Project Safeguard includes, "It is recognized that perpetrators of domestic violence are ultimately responsible for the death of victims. Thus, the goal of this committee is not to place blame but rather to better understand the dynamics of domestic violence when death is involved and thereby diminish the possibilities of future fatalities."

## DEATH REVIEW TEAM PURPOSES AND GOALS

From reviewing existing literature, a common purpose for the existing teams is to better understand, intervene, and prevent domestic homicide.

Family Court Judge Michael Town, Hawaii, hopes review teams will:

1. improve communication among the court and agencies in a time of crisis;
2. provide accurate information to others including the media and elected officials;
3. suggest improvements in the multiple systems involved in domestic violence cases.

## SCOPE OF REVIEW

It is clear from review teams across the country that there is considerable variation in terms of which deaths are reviewed. As noted, the Philadelphia Project reviews hundreds of cases, taking perhaps 30 minutes per review.

The idea in Philadelphia is to identify as many cases as possible where women died as a direct or indirect result of domestic violence. Conversely, reviews like the Charan Investigation seek to identify system failures through an extremely detailed analysis of one case. In many ways the Florida fatality review project is intermediate between these two ends of the continuum. Although the Florida study has not conducted public hearings with respect to the cases reviewed, the deaths are scrutinized in great detail using materials from multiple agencies. At the same time the Florida study identified and then reviewed 328 domestic deaths, a number comparable to the Philadelphia undertaking.

As the Florida teams form and begin their review work another recurring theme has been whether to review near fatalities. This concern to review near fatalities has also cropped up elsewhere. One possibility is the formation of a subcommittee or offshoot review body, charged with reviewing incidents where women are severely injured but not killed. Given the fact that witnesses who survive these near-fatal episodes will be severely traumatized the approach to this kind of review raises important ethical questions.

## EDUCATION AND AWARENESS

Another commonly stated goal of teams is to educate the community in general, and women in particular, about the heightened risk of lethal domestic violence. Ideally, education may enable victims of domestic violence to make more informed choices about their survival strategies and service providers to assist them more effectively. As Stone points out, "there is a fine line between warning and frightening. The women should not be discouraged from leaving a dangerous situation; they should be assisted in developing a safety plan and protected during its implementation." However, given that battered women are often extremely perceptive about men's use of violence and finely attuned to escalations in violence, none of the above should be taken to mean the reason battered women are killed is they are poorly informed of the risks they face. Clearly, as noted elsewhere, batterers are responsible for their violence and the extension of multiple services to battered women in combination with the incapacitation of batterers is the best prevention tool.

## FATALITY REVIEW TEAM MEMBERSHIP

Legislation setting up child fatality review teams is varied in its mandates and recommendations regarding team membership. As Stone indicates, some states did not legislate membership, others required a small number of members, and still others spelled out who members should be or where they should be drawn from.

The discussions about membership of child fatality review teams varied by state. These discussions have informed the debate about membership of adult review teams. Usually adult fatality review teams are inclusive rather than exclusive, often being open to incorporating new members and agencies. With regard to adult review teams, Stone recommends including a member of the public to guard against members engaging in cover-ups. In Nevada, teams must include, without limitation, representatives of organizations concerned with law enforcement, physical and mental health, or the prevention of domestic violence and assistance to victims of domestic violence.

In Delaware, a Fatal Incident Review Team will be co-chaired by two members of the Coordinating Council. In addition to the Chairs, the Review Team shall consist of six other core members: the Attorney General or his or her designee, the Director of the Division of Family Services or his or her designee, the chair of the Domestic Violence Task Force or his or her designee, the Chief Judge of the Family Court or his or her designee, the Chief Magistrate of the Justice of the Peace Courts or his or her designee and a law enforcement officer to be appointed by the Delaware Chiefs of Police Council. The Team can invite other members to serve on an ad hoc basis and participate as full members of the team for a particular review. Such persons may include, but are not limited to, individuals with particular expertise that would be helpful to the review panel, representatives from organizations or agencies that had contact with or provided services to the individual prior to his or her death, that individual's abusive partner or family member, or the alleged perpetrator of the death.

Under California Penal Code 11163.3 (d1-11) domestic violence death review teams shall be comprised of, but not limited to, the following:

1. Experts in the field of forensic pathology.
2. Medical personnel with expertise in domestic violence abuse.
3. Coroners and medical examiners.
4. Criminologists.
5. District attorneys and city attorneys.
6. Domestic violence shelter service staff and battered women's advocates.
7. Law enforcement personnel.
8. Representatives of local agencies that are involved with domestic violence abuse reporting.
9. County health department staff who deal with domestic violence victims' health issues.
10. Representatives of local child abuse agencies.
11. Local professional associations of persons described in 1-10.

The California legislation still allows for local discretion around the construction of teams. Since the originating agency is not restricted by the legislation, each county is free to decide upon the convening agency. Alana Bowman recommends that several advocates for battered women be included in the makeup of the teams to assure that the perspectives of victims are incorporated into social policy. Given the importance of appreciating the perspectives of underserved populations, it might also be useful to have advocates who have experience working with abused minority women, the elderly, women from rural communities, and disabled women.

Although membership patterns vary slightly from state to state, the core of the teams seems to be drawn from three main arenas: public health; criminal justice; and, advocacy/ social services. I refer readers to the appendices for these minor variations by state.

## DEATH REVIEW TEAM PROTOCOLS

In the case of child fatality review teams, participants tended to organize locally and engage in face-to-face deliberations. Except for Georgia, all states which pioneered child teams put them under the auspices of an existing agency or state official. The early legislation establishing child death review teams did not delineate specific activities, duties, and protocols for those teams. Rather, local teams worked out these issues. Later legislation benefited from these pioneering activities and the work of subsequent teams was more closely specified.

A number of adult domestic violence fatality review teams have produced interagency agreements that facilitate the sharing of information and otherwise assist with the collation, coordination, and synthesis of data from each agency.

Under California Penal Code s 11163.3 (c) a county can develop a protocol that may be used as a guideline to assist coroners and other persons who perform autopsies on domestic violence victims to determine whether domestic violence contributed to death or whether domestic violence had occurred prior to death, but was not the actual cause of death.

The Washington State Project highlights two models for death reviews: the "Investigative Fatality Review" and the "Systems Analysis Fatality Review." The "investigative model" prioritizes the need to identify domestic violence fatalities which have not previously been identified as domestic violence related by police, prosecutors, and coroners. Its goals include understanding how or why deaths were not classified as domestic violence related and working toward clearer elucidation of causes of death. In particular, the investigative reviews make much of the need to improve protocols for coroners and others investigating deaths. If this is achieved then the outcome will be not only a more accurate count of domestic violence related deaths, but also an increase in public awareness of domestic violence as a threat to life and well-being. The "systems approach" prioritizes the need to identify how interventions were ineffective. The goal is to change the policies and procedures of involved agencies. Under this model, it is not necessary to identify every domestic violence related death.

## CONFIDENTIALITY, LIABILITY AND IMMUNITY

This section introduces a complex set of issues that will be discussed at great length at the Domestic Violence Fatality Reviews: A National Summit, in Key West, October 1998. The information below is not designed to present definitive positions on confidentiality, liability, and immunity. Rather it is anticipated that jurisdictions will move toward resolving these issues and concerns in their own way.

Among child fatality review teams, Minnesota was one of the first states to address the confidentiality issue. Under the Minnesota Statute, the team has access to confidential (non-public) information if maltreatment is thought to have contributed to the death. This includes private hospital records. This confidential information is not subject to subpoena or discovery. Neither can the deliberations at the Minnesota team meetings be disclosed, unless disclosure furthers the process of reviewing the death.

Regarding adult domestic violence fatality review, a small number of states have addressed issues regarding confidentiality, liability, and immunity. In Nevada, information can be shared among team members regarding the decedent or any person who was in contact with the victim and any other information deemed by the team to be pertinent to the review. This information is to remain confidential. In addition, each member of the team is immune from civil or criminal liability for an activity related to the review of the death. Those related to the decedent within the third degree of consanguinity may receive a report of the domestic fatality from the team.

In Delaware, the review process, and any records created by it, shall be exempt from the provisions of the Freedom of Information Act in Chapter 100 of Title 29. All records and documents contributing to the formulation of reviews are deemed confidential. Such records and documents are not subject to subpoena or discovery. Team members will not be required to make any statements regarding review deliberations. Likewise members and their agents will be immune from claims and not be subject to any suits, liability, damages or any other recourse, civil or criminal, arising from any act, proceeding, decision or determination undertaken or performed or recommendation made, provided such persons acted in good faith and without malice in carrying out their responsibilities; good faith and lack of malice are presumed and the burden of proving otherwise falls upon the complainant.

In Maine, persons disclosing or providing information or records upon the request of the panel are not criminally or civilly liable for disclosing or providing information or records in compliance with this paragraph. The proceedings and records of the panel are confidential and are not subject to subpoena, discovery or introduction into evidence in a civil or criminal action. The commission shall disclose conclusions of the review panel upon request, but may not disclose information, records or data that are otherwise classified as confidential.

Other teams have required team members to sign statements saying they will not disclose confidential information. Under this arrangement case-identifying information with agency identifiers can only be removed from team meetings by the agency contributing the information.

Immunity laws may be required to insulate team members from personal liability stemming from their participation in death reviews. States may want to pass laws to protect team members. However, the consensus seems to be that the risk of personal liability is minimal.

## CONDUCTING THE REVIEW: SOME PRACTICAL CONSIDERATIONS

Alana Bowman has identified a number of possible steps involved in creating review teams mentioned below:

a. Decide upon an agency to house the project, send out notices, gather information, and generate reports.
b. Identify key agencies and their possible representatives and alternates.
c. Require everyone involved to sign confidentiality agreements, both individually and on behalf of their agencies.
d. Define goals, purposes, etc. of team.
e. Develop procedures and protocols for what the team will review.
f. Select cases to review.
g. Have team members conduct reviews of their own agency involvement in a case and contribute this information when team review convenes. The team can then synthesize respective contributions into an overall review.
h. Summarize review.
i. Decide upon dissemination of review findings.
j. Develop aggregate data from many reviews and decide upon public dissemination and formatting.

Team members will likely review the deaths in their respective agencies and bring those findings to the death review team. Protocols need to be established regarding the timing of the review, producing reports, disseminating information, etc. Most existing teams examine domestic violence-related deaths in which there are/were romantic links between the parties (e.g. Santa Clara County, Washington State). It seems that teams have paid less attention to phenomena such as the killings between men stemming from competition over women. Another key issue is whether to review open or closed cases. Research in Florida reveals that reviewing cases pending prosecution is problematic because the state is unwilling or unable to share information that might compromise a conviction. Most known teams find closed cases ideal to review. Alana Bowman suggests that for teams starting their review work it is best to review homicide-suicides in which the perpetrator is clearly identified and there is no prosecution pending.

Existing teams have varying powers regarding the acquisition of information. In Florida, teams are discussing the feasibility of bringing in witnesses to improve understanding of domestic deaths. Other states have formally empowered teams in this area.

For example, the Delaware review team has the power and authority to administer oaths and to compel the attendance of witnesses whose testimony is related to the death under review. It can also compel the production of records related to the death by filing a praecipe for a subpoena, through the office of the Attorney General, with the Prothonotary of any county.

## CHANGING POLICIES

### Monitoring Change

Policy changes have developed as a result of team activity. The San Francisco Task Force investigating the Charan case suggested that an independent task force be established to monitor the implementation of the Charan investigation recommendations. Under the medical model, mortality reviews are themselves reviewed. First, causes of death are scrutinized. Second, the review process is assessed by a central body under the broad umbrella of "Quality Assurance". This review of the reviews can occur on an annual basis.

Delaware review teams must issue annual reports to the Domestic Violence Coordinating Council summarizing in aggregate fashion all findings and recommendations made over the preceding year. The summaries must note any systemic changes introduced as a result of review work. The commission shall disclose conclusions of the review panel upon request, but may not disclose information, records or data that are otherwise classified as confidential.

The Maine Commission shall submit a report on the panel's activities, conclusions, and recommendations to the joint standing committee of the Legislature having jurisdiction over judiciary matters by January 1, 1999, and annually thereafter.

**Typical recommendations for change include:**

- Disseminating information to victims of domestic violence so that they can make more informed choices regarding risk of lethal violence, leaving violent men, etc..
- Educating the public through agencies such as schools and the media. For example, the Santa Clara County report recommends all school districts develop a curriculum which addresses domestic violence.
- Producing user-friendly screening mechanisms for advocates, the courts, law enforcement, social service providers, attorneys, child protection workers, medical/ public health personnel, etc..
- Creating a greater awareness of the links between workplace violence and domestic violence. The Santa Clara County team notes that seven of its 51 deaths occurred in the workplace.

## RECOMMENDATIONS FROM THE FLORIDA MORTALITY REVIEW REPORT

1. That systematic data on domestic fatalities be collected from multiple sources in order to better identify, statistically weigh, and as a consequence, prioritize the correlates of domestic fatalities. These correlates may then be used across agencies for awareness and sensitivity training and also as crucial frames of reference for intervening in those domestic violence episodes that present the threat of lethality. This will never be a foolproof science. However, a system of red flags based on systematic data may provide a simple and user-friendly means of assessing danger.
2. That the reporting of domestic fatalities to Florida Department of Law Enforcement should contain the names of the victims in addition to the demographic and impersonal minutiae currently available. Additionally, the report recommends that reporting agencies code their domestic fatalities more carefully, remaining cognizant of the statutory definition of domestic violence.

3. That police agencies who provide a wealth of important and useful information on domestic fatalities go several steps further and investigate whether or not red flags or warning signs existed prior to fatalities. It is crucial to be able to see clearly from a domestic violence report the history of prior violence, police involvement, injunctions, prior criminal histories, any obsessively possessive behavior, mental illness, separation pending in the relationship, etc.. At some point there must be some kind of screening mechanism or instrument that identifies high risk cases before fatalities occur. Once this identification has occurred then plans need to be made for unusual and highly proactive police/judicial/social services interventions.
4. That improved access be given to data on child fatalities.
5. That much more multiagency coordination and cooperation need to take place to protect women better. Twenty-two women were killed in domestic fatalities in the state of Florida in 1994 while in possession of an injunction. Clearly, issuing injunctions without providing other important supports and protection for battered women is not enough. Much work remains to be done to intervene in pre-lethal situations to prevent further escalation.
6. Those agencies within jurisdictions work together to review domestic (adult and child) fatalities. However, this review should be more than a social post-mortem. Rather the review should set in motion those strategies that interagency teams can use to prevent fatalities. The report recommends transcending the rhetoric of blame and shame, and bringing agencies to the table. This does not mean that agencies should not be held accountable for their negligence or malfeasance. Rather the report strongly recommends the carefully planned and gradual establishment of fatality review teams in selected jurisdictions in Florida.

## RECOMMENDATIONS FROM THE KENTUCKY ATTORNEY GENERAL'S REPORT, 1993

The recommendations promoted the establishment of county-level domestic violence councils. These interagency councils should develop, coordinate, and strengthen local criminal justice and community service responses to domestic violence. In particular with regard to the potential for lethal violence, these interagency councils should work to better protect women who decide to leave violent relationships.

## OTHER RECOMMENDATIONS

A number of child fatality review teams have identified the need to provide grief counseling for the surviving family members of the decedent. This seems particularly pressing in the case of children whose parents are killed in domestic violence homicides, or who survive attempted domestic homicides themselves. As Jerry Adler notes, children should be encouraged to grieve, express their feelings of fear, loss, and anger. Particularly vulnerable according to some experts are children aged 9-13 who are moving toward independence and who may be less likely to share their emotions publicly. Children who witness parental homicides are emotionally traumatized, stigmatized, and deeply scarred by such a terrifying incident. According to Sondra Burman and Paula Allen-Meares, these children exhibit debilitating symptoms comparable to post traumatic stress disorder (PTSD). These authors describe the behavioral and expressive therapeutic treatment strategies used to assist two child victims.

The Courts and Communities: Confronting Violence in the Family Conference Highlights Document, San Francisco (1993), noted the importance of awareness of lethality issues in the disposition of domestic cases. The Highlights Document raises important questions about children's safety and makes the basic point that "children are safer when moms are safer." Regarding issues of safety in the courtroom the report identifies red flags for lethal violence (prior use of deadly weapon; separation/estrangement; escalating domestic violence; public violence; threats to kill; stalking; obsessive jealousy; alcohol or drug abuse; sexual abuse; violence toward children; suicide attempts; hostage-taking). Specifically the report notes "because a domestic homicide is often preceded by numerous contacts with the justice system, developing better information systems and communications among courts, law enforcement and prosecution is an important way to reduce the risk of lethal violence." There are also brief but useful notes on pretrial release issues, courtroom security, accelerated dockets/special dockets, and case coordination.

## NEW YORK COMMISSION

The Report of the New York Commission recommends that:

- Coordinated safety plans be developed by victims in conjunction with multiple involved agencies. The plans must take into account the victim's special needs including any issues of health, language, culture, or sexual orientation.
- Medical practitioners are required to report to local police any serious physical injury stemming from the assaultive behavior of another. Three members of the Commission dissented on this point arguing that victims of domestic violence are better served by a combination of domestic violence counseling, safety planning, and referral at a hospital, than by mandatory reporting by the hospital or doctor.
- Existing requirements that hospitals and diagnostic treatment facilities document and offer referrals to victims of domestic violence to all medical practitioners be extended. Records of confirmed or suspected domestic violence currently required to be noted in a patient's chart medical staff be reported on an anonymous basis to the New York State Department of Health to provide data for research and policy development.
- The New York Criminal Procedure Law and Family Court Act be amended to expand the definition of family or household to include cohabiting couples, same-sex couples, and dating couples.
- Sole or joint custody of a child not to be granted to perpetrators of domestic violence. If visitation is granted then it should be supervised (no recommendations are made as to the nature of that supervision or any indication

of security arrangements or training in domestic violence issues for supervisory staff).

- The New York Penal Code be amended to provide that commission of domestic violence is sufficient grounds for a charge and conviction for Endangering the Welfare of a child.
- Child protection and adult advocacy services are coordinated.
- New York Criminal Procedure Law be amended to provide that prosecutors can appeal bail determinations and lenient sentences; and that the criteria for bail determinations be expanded to include: the issuance of prior orders of protection against the defendant; the violation of any court order by the defendant; the defendant's history, if any, of prior domestic violence or threats of violence; and other circumstances that would show a propensity to harm the victim or others.
- New York Criminal Procedure Law be amended to permit the introduction of a witness's prior testimony as direct evidence, if it is inconsistent with the witness's testimony at trial and if the declarant is subject to cross-examination; and to broaden the exceptions to the hearsay rule in New York for present sense impressions and excited utterances.
- Police departments be allowed to either confiscate or accept the surrender of any handguns or long guns if the owner is arrested, the subject of an order of protection, if the incident involves the use or threatened use of force, or if the officer reasonably believes that the presence of the weapon at the scene creates imminent risk of violence or serious physical injury.
- Employers are responsible for developing strategies to enhance the safety of domestic violence victims in the workplace. See for example the policy adopted by Merrill Lynch to protect its employees who are victimized by domestic violence.
- Review of availability of shelters, funding levels for shelters, and nature of service delivery is conducted.

- Broad public education programs be instituted in schools, faith communities, workplaces, and other community organizations.
- A state fatality review board not is established at this time. However, local communities to review their own fatalities on an as-need-to basis, with the possibility of a state review board being established at some later date.

# 5

# The Enforcing Court Full Faith and Credit

## FULL FAITH AND CREDIT

Since 1994, the Violence Against Women Act's full faith and credit provision (18 U.S.C. & sect; 2265) has required every jurisdiction in the United States to recognize and enforce valid protection orders. These jurisdictions include:

- A state and its political subdivisions
- A tribal government
- The District of Columbia
- A commonwealth, territory or possession of the United States. (American Samoa, Guam, Northern Mariana Islands, Puerto Rico, and U.S. Virgin Islands)

## ELEMENTS OF AN ENFORCEABLE ORDER

- The respondent is given notice and an opportunity to be heard, or, in the case of an *ex parte* order, the respondent will be given notice and an opportunity to be heard within a reasonable time, consistent with the requirements of due process.
- The issuing court had personal and subject matter jurisdiction to issue the order.
- The order has not expired.
- A protection order from another jurisdiction that has these elements must be afforded a presumption of enforceability.

## MUTUAL ORDERS

Mutual orders are fully enforceable against the respondent. Provisions against the petitioner are not entitled to interstate/tribal enforcement if:

- No cross or counter petition, complaint, or other written pleading was filed by the respondent seeking such a protection order; or
- A cross or counter petition has been filed and the court did not make specific findings that each party was entitled to such an order.

## FACILITATING PROTECTION

- Communicate with the issuing court to clear up ambiguities, verify validity, establish the status of service, etc.
- Be aware that some state and tribal laws impose additional requirements beyond VAWA. For example, VAWA requires enforcement of out of state and tribal orders, but does not require registration, as a few state statutes do.
- Notify protected parties of the National Domestic Violence Hotline number.

## ENFORCING PROTECTION ORDERS OF OTHER JURISDICTIONS

A. Enforce the terms of the order, even if the enforcing jurisdiction would have no authority to enter such terms, as in cases where:

- Category of protected persons would not be eligible for relief in enforcing jurisdiction;
- Order contains relief unavailable in enforcing jurisdiction;
- Order has longer duration than provided for in enforcing jurisdiction; or
- Order calls for surrender of weapons and enforcing jurisdiction has no such provision.

B. Use the enforcement procedures of the enforcing jurisdiction.

- Treat the violation as a criminal offense if it is criminalized in the enforcing jurisdiction.
- Award attorney's fees if sought and if provided for in enforcing jurisdiction.

## FIREARMS CONSIDERATIONS

In addition to any state, tribal or territorial laws on firearms, certain federal firearms restrictions may apply in some protection order cases.

- A defendant may not obtain, possess or transport a firearm or ammunition for the duration of the qualifying protection order.
- A defendant who has been convicted of a qualifying misdemeanor crime of domestic violence may not possess a firearm or ammunition.
- It may be a crime to sell or otherwise dispose of a firearm or ammunition to any person known to be prohibited from obtaining or possessing a firearm.

## CRAFTING AN ENFORCEABLE ORDER

- Use clear and concise language in a legible order. For example, when crafting visitation provisions, be precise about times, location, persons and duration, and avoid vague and unenforceable terms such as "reasonable."
- State in the order that the respondent had notice and opportunity to be heard.
- Comply with the Parental Kidnapping Prevention Act (PKPA) and the Uniform Child Custody Jurisdiction Act (UCCJA) or Uniform Child Custody Jurisdiction and Enforcement Act (UCCJEA) for custody and visitation provisions within protection orders.
- Cite the state statute upon which the court's decision and order are based. Provide the court's telephone number and, where available, the state registry telephone number.
- State the duration of the order and its expiration date, if any.
- For a mutual order indicate that a pleading was filed by

each party, and make a written finding that each party is entitled to protection.

## FACILITATING PROTECTION

- Inform the parties orally and in writing that the order is enforceable in all 50 states, U.S. territories, tribal lands and the District of Columbia. Inform the parties that they should not assume other courts or counsel are familiar with full faith and credit.
- Indicate in writing or certify on the order that the order complies with VAWA's full faith and credit provision (18 U.S.C. § 2265) and meets the definition under U.S.C. & sect; 2266.
- Provide the protected parties certified copies of the order and advise them to keep one with them at all times.
- Indicate on the face of the order whether there has been reasonable notice and opportunity to be heard. It is good practice to have the respondent, if present, sign an acknowledgment of service on the face of the order.
- State that violation of the order, in addition to any state or tribal sanctions, may subject the respondent to prosecution for such federal crimes as:
- Firearms possession
- Interstate travel to commit domestic violence
- Interstate stalking
- Interstate violation of a domestic violence order.
- At the request of the enforcing court, consult to clear up ambiguities, verify validity, establish the status of service, etc.
- Notify the protected party of the National Domestic Violence Hotline number.

In addition to any state, tribal or territorial laws on firearms, certain federal firearms restrictions apply in some protection order cases.

- A defendant may not obtain, possess or transport a firearm or ammunition for the duration of the qualifying protection order.

- A defendant who has been convicted of a qualifying misdemeanor crime of domestic violence may not possess a firearm or ammunition.
- It may be a crime to sell or otherwise dispose of a firearm or ammunition to any person known to be prohibited from obtaining or possessing a firearm.
- To facilitate enforcement of the federal firearms restrictions, include in the order the specific findings regarding the grounds for issuing the order.

## FULL FAITH AND CREDIT JUDGE'S BENCH CARD

## PROTECTION ACROSS JURISDICTIONS: FULL FAITH & CREDIT LAWS AND ENFORCEMENT

18 U.S.C. & Sect; 2265: Full Faith and Credit Given to Protection Orders

a. Full faith and credit. Any protection order issued that is consistent with subsection (b) of this section by the court of one State or Indian tribe (the issuing State or Indian tribe) shall be accorded full faith and credit by the court of another State or Indian tribe (the enforcing State or Indian tribe) and enforced as if it were the order of the enforcing State or tribe.

b. Protection order. A protection order issued by a State or tribal court is consistent with this subsection if -

   1. Such court has jurisdiction over the parties and matter under the law of such State or Indian tribe; and

   2. Reasonable notice and opportunity to be heard is given to the person against whom the order is sought sufficient to protect that person's right to due process. In the case of *ex parte* orders, notice and opportunity to be heard must be provided within the time required by State or tribal law, and in any event within a reasonable time after the order is issued, sufficient to protect the respondent's due process rights.

c. Cross or counter petition. A protection order issued by a State or tribal court against one who has petitioned, filed a complaint, or otherwise filed a written pleading for protection against abuse by a spouse or intimate partner is not entitled to full faith and credit if -

1. no cross or counter petition or complaint, or other written pleading was filed seeking such a protection order; or
2. a cross or counter petition has been filed and the court did not make specific findings that each party was entitled to such an order.

## ORDER OF PROTECTION

Under VAWA (18 U.S.C. & sect;2266), a protection order "includes any injunction or other order issued for the purpose of preventing violent or threatening acts or harassment against, or contact or communication with or physical proximity to, another person, including temporary and final orders issued by civil and criminal courts (other than support or child custody orders) whether obtained by filing an independent action or as a penden te lite order in another proceeding so long as any civil order was issued in response to a complaint, petition or motion filed by or on behalf of a person seeking protection."

## INTENT OF THE LAW

For Victims

- Cross-jurisdictional protection afforded by valid protection orders.

For Abusers

- Cross-jurisdictional accountability for violation of valid protection orders.

For Judges

- Interstate recognition and enforcement of the valid protection orders they enter.
- Endorsement of valid protection orders they may encounter from other jurisdictions.

## TRIBAL ORDERS

The full faith and credit provision applies to orders issued by tribal courts. State courts are required to recognize and enforce valid tribal court orders of protection.

## CRIMINAL PROTECTION ORDERS

The full faith and credit provision applies to valid criminal orders of protection. Generally issued as a condition of release, probation, or parole, such orders may be difficult to enforce because of verification problems and because of a lack of arrest authority in the enforcing jurisdiction.

The issuing court should determine whether extradition is necessary. The enforcing jurisdiction should respond to underlying crimes committed in the jurisdiction.

Consider issuing a free-standing civil or criminal protection order to avoid potential problems.

## CHILD CUSTODY

The courts should act to protect the safety and welfare of the children of either party.

If the enforcing state court has jurisdiction over custody matters and:

- The protection order contains custody or visitation provisions and complies with the parental Kidnapping Prevention Act (PKPA) and the issuing state's Uniform Child Custody Jurisdiction Act (UCCJA) or Uniform Child Custody Jurisdiction and Enforcement Act (UCCJEA) provisions, the court should enforce the protection order.
- The protection order is silent on custody or visitation, the court should accept emergency jurisdiction if permitted by its state UCCJA/UCCJEA provisions and proceed pursuant to those provisions.
- The protection order contains custody or visitation provisions and complies with the PKPA and UCCJA/ UCCJEA, and the petitioner seeks modification based on

a change of circumstances, the court should accept emergency jurisdiction if permitted by its UCCJA/ UCCJEA provisions and proceed pursuant to those provisions.

If the enforcing court does not have jurisdiction over custody matters, the judge should act to protect the children and refer the custody and visitation issues to the appropriate state court for disposition.

## SIMPLY STATED, FULL FAITH AND CREDIT

A valid order of protection is enforceable where it is issued and in all other jurisdictions. This includes all 50 states, Indian tribal lands, the District of Columbia, the U.S. Virgin Islands, Puerto Rico, American Samoa, the Northern Mariana Islands and Guam.

Under the federal Violence Against Women Act (VAWA), jurisdictions must give full faith and credit to valid orders of protection issued by other jurisdictions. Full faith and credit is a legal term that means jurisdictions must honor and enforce orders issued by courts in other jurisdictions.

"Any protection order issued that is consistent with subsection (b) of this section by the court of one State or Indian tribe (the issuing State or Indian tribe) shall be accorded full faith and credit by the court of another State or Indian tribe (the enforcing State or Indian tribe) and enforced as if it were the order of the enforcing State or tribe." 18 U.S.C. sect 2265. What does this mean for survivors of abuse?

For the order of protection to be valid, it must meet the following conditions:

- The court that issued the order must have had personal jurisdiction over the parties and subject matter jurisdiction over the case
- The respondent must have had notice and an opportunity to be heard.* 18 U.S.C. sect 2265(b).

Full faith and credit helps to protect freedom of movement by requiring the justice system to enforce orders of protection throughout the country. If an abuser travels across state or tribal lines and violates a protection order, the abuser can be punished under the laws of the jurisdiction where the violation occurred and also may be charged with federal crimes.

## SURVIVORS OF ABUSE

The full faith and credit provision of VAWA can enable survivors of abuse to call on law enforcement officers and the courts to enforce their orders of protection across state or tribal lines.

When survivors cross jurisdictional lines to work, travel, or relocate, they often find themselves in on-going danger, since frequently they are pursued or stalked by their abusers. For this reason, VAWA establishes nationwide enforcement of orders of protection.

## FULL FAITH AND CREDIT MEAN FOR ABUSERS

The full faith and credit provision of VAWA requires police and courts in the enforcing jurisdiction to treat the order as if it were issued in their own state or tribe.

This means that if the abuser violates the order, he/she can be arrested and prosecuted if the laws of the enforcing jurisdiction allow this type of enforcement for violations of protection orders.

Tribes do not have criminal jurisdiction over non-Indians. Tribal police do have authority to stop, detain and transport non-Indian offenders to state or federal authorities who have criminal jurisdiction over non-Indian crimes. In addition, some tribes use their civil laws to impose civil fines or orders of exclusion to escort non- Indian abusers off tribal lands.

## FULL FAITH AND CREDIT MEAN FOR ADVOCATES

Full faith and credit may be a passport to safety for many survivors of domestic violence so advocates need to be familiar with the federal law and understand how it is being implemented in states and tribes throughout the country. Advocates need to share this information with all survivors.

Advocates also need to advise survivors of the dangers they may face when traveling and assist them with appropriate safety planning.

Abusers who are determined and willing to cross state or tribal lines in pursuit of their victims may be among the most dangerous. With information about full faith and credit, survivors can make more informed decisions about safety.

## ASSESSING DANGER

Factors to consider in determining serious danger/ lethality:

- Separation of the parties
- Threats of homicide/suicide
- Possession or access to weapons
- Stalking
- Obsessive or desperate attachment to victim
- Destruction of victim's property
- History of domestic violence and violent criminal conduct
- Drug or alcohol involvement
- Depression or other mental illness
- Abuse of animals

## SAFETY PLANNING

Advocates should assist survivors in developing a safety plan. Safety plans should be detailed, specific, and practical. Issues to address include:

- Custody and visitation and legal assistance in these matters
- Plans to leave the jurisdiction
- Travel safety
- Getting a protection order that will be enforceable across jurisdictions
- Phone numbers for domestic violence programs, law enforcement, court clerks, and technical assistance

## ORDERS OF PROTECTION ENFORCEABLE

Under VAWA, a protection order is defined as: "any injunction or other order issued for the purpose of preventing violent or threatening acts or harassment against, or contact or communication with, or physical proximity to, another person, including temporary and final orders issued by civil and criminal courts (other than support or child custody orders)..." 18 U.S.C. sect 2266.

The full faith and credit provision applies to both civil and criminal orders of protection, whether issued ex parte, after a hearing, or by agreement. Orders may differ from jurisdiction to jurisdiction in form, content, length, layout, or name (e.g., protection from abuse order, no contact order, stay away order, harassment order, restraining order, permanent order, conditions of release order).

## ORDERS OF PROTECTION ENFORCEABLE

Civil Orders of ProtectionConsent Orders. If a valid order of protection is issued on behalf of only one party, the federal law does not require that the order include a specific finding of abuse to be enforceable across jurisdictional lines. This means that if the victim files a petition for an order of protection and the abuser consents or agrees to the entry of the order, even without admitting to the abuse, the order will still be entitled to full faith and credit.

Mutual Orders. Sometimes an order of protection will contain a mutual "no contact" provision or it will direct both parties not to abuse each other. The full faith and credit section of VAWArequires special safeguards for enforcement of this type of order across jurisdictional lines. It states that an order should be enforced against the respondent and not the petitioner, unless the respondent cross filed a written pleading for an order of protection and the issuing court made a specific finding that each party had abused the other. If such findings were made, the order may be enforced against both parties. 18 U.S.C. sect 2265(c).

Custody Provisions. Orders of protection often include terms that award custody of the minor children to the victim. However, the definition of "protection order" in sect 2266 of VAWA contains language that specifically excludes custody and support orders from court orders that are entitled to interstate enforcement under full faith and credit. It is unclear whether Congress intended to exclude the custody provisions in orders of protection or only custody orders that are part of separate divorce or custody decrees. Until this issue is clarified, advocates should look to other state, tribal, and federal laws that govern custody and visitation orders to try to determine if a custody order can be enforced in other jurisdictions. Some of the federal laws to check include the Uniform Child Custody Jurisdiction Act (UCCJA), the Uniform Child Custody Jurisdiction and Enforcement Act (UCCJEA), the Parental Kidnapping Prevention Act (PKPA), and the Indian Child Welfare Act (ICWA). If a custody provision in an order of protection meets the jurisdictional requirements of either the UCCJA or UCCJEA of the issuing jurisdiction and the PKPA, it is entitled to interstate enforcement. These laws can be quite complex, so advocates should encourage survivors to seek legal assistance.

You can assist abused persons in their efforts to protect their children in the following ways:

- Assist the survivor in getting legal representation many legal services programs provide direct representation and legal assistance. The Battered Women's Justice Project (Civil) at 903-0111 ext. 2 offers information on how to obtain legal representation.
- If the order meets the requirements of the UCCJEA or UCCJA and PKPA, request that the court include a statement to that effect in the order of protection
- Assist the survivor in getting a trusted friend, battered women's program representative, or attorney to accept service if the abuser makes an effort to change the order of protection or seeks a separate custody order after the survivor leaves the jurisdiction

- Remind judges and policy makers of the importance of protecting the children of abused persons and the fact that abusers often use children to control their partners

Criminal Orders of Protection. The full faith and credit provision of VAWA applies to valid criminal orders of protection. These orders may be part of pre-trial release orders, conditional release orders or probation orders. They also may be separate, independent orders. Enforcement across state or tribal lines may be problematic, because the way to enforce such orders usually requires a hearing before the court that issued the order. Jurisdictions vary in the type of authority given to police officers to make arrests without a warrant for violations of criminal orders. Few states and tribes have separate provisions in their criminal laws for violation of such orders. If a criminal order is violated across state or tribal lines, the enforcing jurisdiction can probably only hold the perpetrator for extradition, which is a formal legal process to send the offender back to the home (issuing) jurisdiction. Extradition is unlikely to occur when the underlying charge is a misdemeanor crime. Jurisdictions also vary considerably in providing notice to the victim about the existence of criminal orders of protection. Additionally, many criminal orders of protection are not entered into the jurisdiction's protective order registry, so police officers may not be able to obtain confirmation of the order.

Military Orders of Protection.The federal law does not explicitly cover orders of protection issued on military bases or installations. In fact, most military orders will not meet the requirements for validity under VAWAsince they are usually issued by a commanding officer without providing the respondent with an opportunity to be heard. This means that military orders of protection are generally not entitled to full faith and credit. The question that remains is whether military bases are required to enforce orders of protection issued by state or tribal courts. Commanding officers on some bases are directing military police (MPs) to enforce civilian (state or tribal) orders of protection issued against service members. Such enforcement usually consists of informing the local civilian courts or law enforcement agency of the violation and assisting the civilian authorities in investigating and prosecuting the violation in civilian court.

## FEDERAL LAW BEING IMPLEMENTED

At present, there is considerable variation among jurisdictions regarding implementation procedures. Some have enacted full faith and credit laws to implement VAWAwhile others have developed enforcement protocols. Advocates need to be familiar with full faith and credit legislation and procedures in their own jurisdictions as well as those of neighboring jurisdictions so they can provide accurate information to survivors.

### Registration/Filing

The federal law does not require registration or filing of orders of protection, however, a handful of jurisdictions require registration for purposes of enforcement.

Benefits. Registration/filing may be necessary to ensure full faith and credit if it is required by state or tribal law. Registration may also help to facilitate proper enforcement by courts and law enforcement agencies. These procedures, however, are relatively new in many jurisdictions so clerks of court and law enforcement personnel may be unfamiliar with how to register or file an order. Advocates should be prepared to assist survivors, if appropriate, in complying with registration or filing procedures.

Risks. Registration is not without risks. Filing can be dangerous in certain situations, especially if the abused person is registering the order in a jurisdiction where notice is sent to the abuser or where an order of protection is deemed a public record. It would be time-consuming and difficult, but a diligent abuser could locate the victim by searching court records throughout the jurisdiction. Advocates need to advise survivors who want to keep their whereabouts confidential that registration may be risky.

Registration/filing may not always be practical or even possible. In an emergency, there may not be an opportunity to register or file the order before seeking enforcement.

Recognition. The federal law does not require recognition of orders of protection, however, a number of Indian tribes recognize orders from other jurisdictions under the legal principle of comity.

### Certification

A certified copy of an order of protection generally contains a stamp, seal, or signature of the issuing judge or clerk of court and a notation that the copy is an authentic duplicate of the original order of the court. VAWA does not mandate that an order of protection be "certified" to be entitled to enforcement across state, territorial, or tribal lines. Nonetheless, many jurisdictions require that a copy of a foreign order be certified for purposes of registration or filing. Therefore, advocates may want to suggest that survivors get certified copies of their orders of protection to ensure proper enforcement.

## LAW ENFORCEMENT

Law enforcement officers are required to enforce orders of protection from other jurisdictions in the same manner they enforce orders issued within their own jurisdictions.

Before arresting for violation of an order of protection issued in another jurisdiction, officers should verify that a valid order exists, determine whether the order was violated, and enforce the terms of the order pursuant to the laws of the enforcing jurisdiction (e.g. arrest if probable cause exists and if the alleged violation is an arrestable offense).

Tribal police (unless they have been cross-deputized or crosscommissioned) do not have authority to arrest non-Indians. Many tribes call in the city, county, or state law enforcement officers to make those types of arrests.

As federal officers, Bureau of Indian Affairs (BIA) officers DO have criminal jurisdiction over non-Indians who commit offenses against Indians, and they exercise that jurisdiction in coordination with the FBI and U.S. Attorneys' offices. The BIA sometimes deputizes qualified tribal police officers who assist in exercising this jurisdiction.

State, Tribal and Local Electronic Protection Order Registries. Many states, tribes, and localities have developed computerized databases that contain records of valid orders of protection issued or registered within the jurisdiction. Some jurisdictions also keep records of expired orders. If a state or tribal registry is accurate and up-to-date, it can be accessed to verify the existence of a protection order in cases where the victim cannot produce a paper copy or where the paper copy does not appear to be valid. It should be noted that not all states and tribes have centralized databases of protection orders so officers should be prepared to take other steps to check the validity of an order.

The NCIC Protection Order File. In 1997, the FBI established the National Crime Information Center's (NCIC) Protection Order File. Because state and tribal participation is voluntary and NCIC requires certain data elements to list an order, the national registry does not contain orders from all jurisdictions. As such, the NCIC Protection Order File is an imperfect verification tool. Law enforcement officers who access the national registry to confirm the status of an order need to be aware of its limitations. In particular, advocates should remind officers that:

- Many states and tribes are not yet participating in the FBI registry
- Even if a state or tribe enters orders into the NCIC system, checking the NCIC file or verifying with the state registry may not result in a positive verification for reasons including the following:
- the data fields in some state or tribal registries may be incomplete or incompatible with the NCIC file
- registries may not always capture 100% of enforceable orders

- there may be a time delay between the issuance of the order and entry into the state or tribal registry or the NCIC file

## VERIFICATION OF AN ORDER BY A LAW ENFORCEMENT OFFICER

If the survivor has a paper copy of the order, the officer should enforce the order if it:

- Contains the names of both parties
- Includes the date it was issued
- Appears to be in effect (i.e., has not expired)
- Specifies terms and conditions with which the abuser must comply
- Contains the name of the issuing court
- Includes a signature of or on behalf of a judicial officer

If the survivor does not have a paper copy of the order, the officer can:

- Check to see whether the order has been entered into the issuing or enforcing jurisdiction's protection order registry or the NCIC Protection Order File
- Contact the issuing court for verification of the order's validity
- Arrest for all violations of the order and any other crimes that may have been committed
- Alert the prosecutor's office of all crimes committed under the enforcing jurisdiction's criminal code and potential federal domestic violence crimes
- Enforce the protection order based on a good faith belief that the order is valid

## VERIFYING THE TERMS AND CONDITIONS OF AN ORDER OF PROTECTION

Although verification is not required under the federal law, it may be required by the enforcing jurisdiction under certain circumstances (e.g., the victim does not have a copy of the order).

## COURTS

Courts are required to give full faith and credit to orders of protection from other jurisdictions. This means that the order must be enforced as issued, but that the court should apply the laws of the enforcing jurisdiction if the order is violated. To facilitate implementation of full faith and credit:

- Clerks of court should be familiar with the mandates of the federal law and be prepared to file or register an order upon presentation by a survivor
- Judges should
- be familiar with full faith and credit when issuing and enforcing orders of protection
- issue orders that are explicit, clear, comprehensive, and legible
- include language in orders confirming that the requirements for "validity" under VAWA have been met
- include notations in orders that the custody provisions meet the requirements of the UCCJA or UCCJEA and PKPA
- inform both parties orally and in writing that the order is enforceable in all jurisdictions, violations of the order may result in state, tribal, or federal sanctions wherever the violations occur, and enforcement procedures may vary significantly from jurisdiction to jurisdiction
- inform the protected party that laws and procedures vary among the tribes and encourage the protected party to seek further assistance and information on enforcement procedures if he/she plans to travel across tribal lines
- The relief granted by the issuing jurisdiction must be enforced even if such relief is unavailable under the laws of the enforcing jurisdiction
- The laws and penalties of the enforcing jurisdiction must be followed when imposing sanctions for violations of orders
- If there is a challenge to "validity" (e.g., respondent denies receiving notice), the enforcing court should contact the issuing jurisdiction to verify information

- The issuing jurisdiction should be notified of outcomes of any enforcement proceedings in the enforcing jurisdiction

## LOCAL/STATE/TRIBAL/FEDERAL PROSECUTORS

In most instances, local, state and tribal prosecutors will handle violations of orders of protection that occur across jurisdictional lines. Prosecutors should:

- Obtain information from the victim, local law enforcement, and the issuing jurisdiction
- Obtain information about all pending and past convictions
- Prosecute alleged violations in accordance with the procedures and laws of the enforcing jurisdiction
- Work to ensure victim safety

Some violations also may qualify for federal prosecution, since VAWAcreated a number of federal domestic violence crimes. To determine when a case should be referred to the U.S. Attorney's office, local, state, and tribal prosecutors should contact their federal counterparts and establish working relationships. Decisions about whether to try the case in state, tribal, or federal court will depend on a variety of factors, including differences in sentencing options, witness protection, adequacy of local, state, or tribal remedies, and available victim and investigative resources.

## ENFORCING JURISDICTION

- Know the laws and procedures of the jurisdiction
- Work with judges, court clerks, prosecutors, and law enforcement to develop a coordinated response for enforcement of orders issued in other jurisdictions
- Check to make sure that the abused person has certified copies of the order and proof of service, or assist in obtaining them
- Inform the abused person of the laws and procedures of the jurisdiction and provide the information needed for the person to decide whether to register the order

- Remind officers that, in most jurisdictions, the protection order can be enforced on its face regardless of whether it is registered/filed in the jurisdiction or listed in a state protection order database or the NCIC Protection Order File (consult the laws and procedures of your jurisdiction)
- Inform the survivor that she/he may need to take the protection order to the tribal court to be recognized, even if she/he has a protection order issued by another tribe
- Inform the survivor that, if appropriate, she/he should take the tribal protection order to the county, state, or other local jurisdiction for registration
- Encourage state, tribal, and federal prosecutors to work together to ensure the most successful prosecution of interjurisdictional cases
- Develop relationships with federal victim/witness coordinators in order to work together to provide victim safety

## SUMMARY OF FEDERAL CRIMES OF DOMESTIC VIOLENCE

Advocates need to be familiar with the new federal criminal laws that pertain to domestic violence in order to inform victims of options related to federal criminal prosecution. The contact for assessment of potential federal crimes is the U.S. Attorney's office in your district. For the following federal crimes, the law defines State to include: a state of the United States, the District of Columbia, a commonwealth, territory, or possession of the United States.

### Interstate Travel to Commit Domestic Violence - 18 U.S.C. Section 2261

It is a Federal crime for a person to travel interstate, or leave or enter Indian country with the intent to injure, harass or intimidate an intimate partner when in the course of or as a result of the travel the abuser commits a violent crime that causes bodily injury. The abuser must intend to commit the domestic violence at the time of travel. The definition of partner is broad and basically includes a person with whom the abuser has cohabited in an intimate relationship (including a current or former spouse) or a person who has a child in common with the abuser. It is also a Federal crime to cause an intimate partner to cross state lines, or leave or enter Indian country by force, coercion, duress, or fraud if the abuser intentionally inflicts bodily injury on the partner during or as a result of the conduct.

## Interstate Stalking - 18 U.S.C. Sections 2261A

It is a Federal crime to cross a state line with the intent to injure or harass any person if, during the course of or as a result of the travel, the defendant places the person or a member of the person's immediate family in reasonable fear of death or serious bodily injury. It also is a federal crime to stalk another individual within the special maritime or territorial jurisdiction of the United States (which includes federal reservations).The definition of immediate family is broad and includes a spouse, parent, child, sibling and all other household members who are related to the primary victim by blood or marriage.

Interstate Violation of an Order of Protection - 18 U.S.C. Section 2262

This law basically prohibits interstate travel or leaving or entering Indian country with intent to violate a valid protection order that prohibits credible threats of violence, repeated harassment, or bodily injury. The abuser must intend to violate the order at the time of travel and a violation of the order must occur. It is also a federal crime to cause an intimate partner to cross state lines, or to leave or enter Indian country by force, coercion, duress, or fraud, if during or as a result of the conduct, the abuser intentionally inflicts bodily injury on the victim in violation of a valid protection order.

Advocate's Guide Glossary of Terms

Certified - a stamp, seal, or signature of the issuing judge or clerk of court noting that the copy is an authentic duplicate of the original order of the court.

Comity - a legal principle where a sovereign nation decides voluntarily to recognize another jurisdiction's court order.

Consent Order - an order of protection which is issued, usually without a finding (legal conclusion) of abuse, but after the respondent consents or agrees to the entry of the order.

Ex parte Order - an emergency or temporary order issued at the request of the petitioner without first providing notice or a hearing to the respondent.

Indian Child Welfare Act (ICWA) - a law that applies to custody proceedings in state courts involving foster care placement, termination of parental rights, preadoptive placement, and adoptive placement of Indian children. The ICWA may apply to divorces or custody proceedings where custody of the child(ren) is given to a third party. This law is significant because abusers often threaten to use the ICWA against battered women even though the ICWAdoes not apply to custody proceedings between the parents of the child(ren).

Jurisdiction (location) - in this guide, jurisdiction is used most commonly as a general name for the geographic areas impacted by the federal law. This includes all 50 states, Indian tribal lands, the District of Columbia, the U.S. Virgin Islands, Puerto Rico, American Samoa, the Northern Mariana Islands, and Guam.

Issuing Jurisdiction - jurisdiction that grants the order of protection.

Enforcing Jurisdiction - jurisdiction that enforces an order of protection issued by another jurisdiction.

Jurisdiction - can also be used as a legal term to refer to the types of authority that a court may exercise.

Subject Matter Jurisdiction - refers to the authority of a court to hear and determine a particular type of case.

Personal Jurisdiction - refers to the power the court may (or may not) have over the parties involved in a particular case.

Mutual Order - a single order of protection that includes prohibitions against both the petitioner and respondent.

Parental Kidnapping Prevention Act (PKPA) - federal legislation enacted to ensure that jurisdictions honor and enforce custody orders entered by the courts of other jurisdictions so long as both parties received prior notice and were given a chance to be heard. The PKPAprioritizes home state jurisdiction so other jurisdictions have to defer to orders entered by the jurisdiction where the child lived for the six-month period prior to the filing of the action.

Petitioner - the person who presents a petition to the court requesting an order of protection. Qualifying Misdemeanor - state or federal misdemeanor crime that has as an element the use or attempted use of physical force or the threatened use of a deadly weapon. 18 U.S.C. sect 922(g).

Qualifying Protection Order - protection order that meets the following conditions: (i) the protected party must be a spouse, former spouse, present or former cohabitant with the respondent, parent of common child, or a child of the respondent; (ii) the order must have been entered after a hearing of which the respondent had notice and an opportunity to appear; (iii) the order must include a finding that the respondent represents a credible threat to the protected party or must include an express prohibition against harassment, stalking, or the use of force that would reasonably be expected to cause injury. 18 U.S.C. sect 922(g).

Recognition - the status granted a court order from another jurisdiction after a tribe determines it is enforceable. The tribe then issues its own order granting recognition.

Registration/Filing - refers to a procedure where an order of protection from one jurisdiction is registered or filed with a clerk of court or law enforcement agency in another jurisdiction. In some jurisdictions, the order may be entered into a local or statewide protective order computer registry. Registration usually creates a public record of the order of protection in the enforcing jurisdiction.

Respondent - the person against whom an order of protection is filed or issued.

Tribe - an Indian nation, Indian tribe, or native sovereign nation.

Uniform Child Custody Jurisdiction Act (UCCJA) - a uniform law, enacted with few variations by all of the states, which establishes jurisdiction to render custody orders that are enforceable across jurisdictional boundaries. The UCCJA sets forth four possible bases of jurisdiction without giving priority to any one over the others. Because of this, it is still possible for more than one state at a time to establish jurisdiction over the same parties and facts and for courts to render conflicting orders in the same case. The Act is more than 30 years old and is inconsistent with some provisions of subsequently enacted federal law.

Uniform Child Custody Jurisdiction and Enforcement Act (UCCJEA) - a replacement for the UCCJA currently being considered by the states and already enacted by a few. This Act establishes one jurisdictional base as having priority over the others - the state where the child has lived for the six months prior to the filing of the custody case - and builds in a number of protections for victims of domestic violence not available in the UCCJA. For example, the UCCJEA creates a structure of cooperation among the courts of the competing states so that the victim does not have to return physically to the home state in order to litigate in its courts; more comprehensive emergency jurisdiction in the refuge state; and a greater likelihood that the home state will voluntarily relinquish jurisdiction if it would be unsafe for the victim to litigate there.

## HELPFUL INTERVENTIONS/EFFECTIVE ADVOCACY

## ISSUING JURISDICTION

- If appropriate, assist the survivor in filing a cross petition if the abuser files for an order first.

- Work with the court and the survivor to ensure that the following language is included in the order:
    1. Order is enforceable outside the jurisdiction.
    2. Crossing jurisdictional lines to violate the order may be a federal crime under VAWA.
    3. Custody provisions are made in compliance with the UCCJA or UCCJEA and PKPA.
    4. The court had jurisdiction to issue the order.
    5. The respondent had notice and an opportunity to be heard.
- Work with the court and the survivor to ensure that the order includes a prohibition against firearm possession, if applicable under the laws of the issuing jurisdiction.
- Work with the court and the survivor to ensure that the order includes required data elements for entry into the NCIC Protection Order File.
- Work with the judge to ensure that the terms of the order are clear and specific.
- Assist the abused person in getting proof of service.
- Make sure that the survivor has several certified copies of the order and carries one at all times.
- Inform the survivor about recognition/ comity and assist in checking on procedures of the particular tribal jurisdiction.
- Provide copies of sect 2265 and 2266 of VAWA for the survivor to carry along with the order.
- Get information about the laws and procedures of the enforcing jurisdiction(s).
- Provide names, addresses, and phone numbers of court clerks, local and federal prosecutors, law enforcement, the state coalition, and local battered women's programs in the jurisdiction(s) the abused person may be traveling.
- If the victim has left the issuing jurisdiction, help the victim find someone who will accept service for any future attempts to change the order.

- Help the survivor develop a detailed safety plan.

## ENFORCING JURISDICTION

- Know the laws and procedures of the jurisdiction.
- Work with judges, court clerks, prosecutors and law enforcement to develop a coordinated response to orders issued in other jurisdictions.
- Make sure that the survivor has certified copies of the order and proof of service, or assist in obtaining them.
- Inform the abused person of the laws and procedures of the jurisdiction.
- If registration is optional or mandatory, provide the information needed for the person to decide whether to register the order.
- Remind officers that, in most jurisdictions, the protection order can be enforced on its face regardless of whether it is registered/ filed in the jurisdiction or listed in a state protection order database or the NCIC Protection Order File (consult the laws and procedures of your jurisdiction).
- For custody issues, assist the abused person in getting legal representation.
- Inform survivor that she/he may need to take the protection order to the tribal court to be recognized, even if she/he has a state protection order or a protection order from another tribe.
- Inform survivor that, if appropriate, she/he should take a tribal protection order to the county, state, or other local jurisdiction for registration.
- Develop relationships with federal victim/witness coordinators in order to work together to provide victim safety.

# 6

# Working Effectively with the Police

## INTRODUCTION

In our society, we turn to the police to intervene in violence. We call them for protection: our own, a neighbor's, a stranger's on the street. With the availability of 9/11 emergency dispatches, their presence is often immediate. We believe and trust that they will protect us. Police officers carry the authority to legally remove an assailant, using force to do so if necessary. Police officers initiate the investigation that a prosecutor relies on when bringing a domestic violence case to court.

Historically, however, women who faced violence in their homes could not rely on police protection. Since the larger community saw domestic violence as a private matter, police were trained to respond accordingly. The community and the criminal justice system expected officers to be involved in only the most extreme, isolated cases. Euphemisms for violence reflect this detachment: "family trouble," "domestic dispute," "husband-wife spat," "a domestic." Police training discouraged arrest and state laws prohibited warrantless arrests for misdemeanor crimes. Police were directed to either defuse the situation or attempt to mediate the "dispute," reinforcing a perception of the victim and assailant as equal parties with equal power over each other's behavior.

Victims were left feeling confused and at fault. Having turned to the police for help, they were left blaming themselves for even bothering to call. Battered women turned to police with one set of expectations but the police responded with another, influenced by training and public expectations.

## A VISION FOR CHANGE

For many years, advocates have pushed the criminal justice system to act promptly and fairly to protect battered women. While a system that large does not change easily or quickly, an increased understanding of the dynamics of violence by its practitioners and the public challenge to violence against women have encouraged a new response.

Over the past twenty years, much energy has gone into reshaping police practice. By means of meetings, lawsuits, policies, and legislation, advocates have insisted that police respond to domestic violence as a crime. In a growing number of communities, police in partnership with advocates and other community institutionsare intervening to protect victims, hold assailants accountable, and challenge the social underpinnings of domestic violence.

The strength of this coordinated intervention lies in the consistency and uniformity of its message: physically abusive behavior is against the law, regardless of the relationship between the assailant and the victim. If you are violent toward your partner, the community will hold you accountable through its police, courts, and other institutions.

Police can be active partners in this change, as they are in several pioneering communities.

For example, police now play key roles in the community intervention efforts of Colorado Springs, San Francisco, Duluth (MN), Quincy (MA), Madison (WI), San Diego, and Seattle. In those cities, police have changed when and how they make arrests, conduct investigations, and write reports. They have changed their relationships with and the level of support they provide to prosecutors and victim advocates.

## ADVOCACY

The variety and strength of support offered to battered women has also significantly expanded in the last two decades. As community-based advocates have pushed police, prosecutors, hospitals, and social service agencies to respond to domestic violence, these systems have developed new policies and services.

The title advocate has been applied to a wide range of victim assistance work. We have learned, however, that the alignment of a positionnamely, how and where a practitioner worksinfluences its function and the degree to which it can affect system-wide change. Here, we make a distinction between victim services delivered within a governmental or quasi-governmental system, and advocacy for change from the outside.

Maintaining a voice outside these systems is central to advocacy. Advocacy requires that the needs of battered women, individually and as a class, come first. This purpose can conflict with the interests of the criminal justice system as it focuses on arrest, prosecution, and sentencing.

In an effort to improve law enforcement's understanding of domestic violence, and its response to battered women, advocates have begun to work directly with police, in both coordinated community response projects and on-scene crisis response teams. To maintain their distinct role, advocates must be mindful of the challenges that come with increased police collaboration and partnership. Creating police change, and broader system change, requires that we understand ourselves as advocates: our own attitudes, functions, job structures, and purposes.

## THE CHANGE PROCESS

### Attitudes

Our personal history shapes our response to domestic violence. Whether officer or advocate, our reactions are grounded in our thoughts and experiences about women, men, marriage, relationships, power, control, families, and violence.

Our distinct backgrounds, shaped by race, gender, class, family of origin, friendships, and cultural influences, mold our attitudes and influence our response on the scene. The challenge to police officers and advocates alike is recognizing how these attitudes affect our work.

Policing, for example, remains an overwhelmingly male profession. In 1999, women represented only 14.3% of the officers in larger law enforcement agencies (those having one hundred or more officers). Male officers who enter policing are exposed to the same cultural messages about women and violence as other men. A male officer who arrives at the scene of a domestic violence crime may himself be controlling or violent toward his partner. Or, he may be operating under a cloud of resentment because he believes the new sergeant got the job he competed for "just because she's a woman." He may be one of those officers who believe that women do not belong anywhere in *his* profession. All of these attitudes can influence his response to the call.

For the few women in policing, domestic violence calls may be seen as a no-win situation. If a female officer is isolated within an unsupportive or hostile agency, she may feel pressure to be contemptuous of women who have been battered. She may want to distance herself from other women, particularly those seen as weak and vulnerable enough to be battered. She may resist doing a thorough job on domestic violence cases if those calls are not considered by her peers to be *real* police work. She may live with an abusive partner.

In impoverished and in culturally and racially distinct communities, police action may be characterized by distrust and tension. Battered women may face significant dilemmas when weighing their needs for police protection against the negative impact of police presence in their communities. Officers who live in these communities may feel personal pressure to try to bridge their law enforcement role and their community's negative experience with police.

The unusual strength of the police culture is largely attributable to two factors. First, the stressful and apparently dangerous nature of the police role produces collegiate bonds of considerable strength, as officers feel themselves besieged in an essentially hostile world. Second, the long hours and the rotating shifts kill most prospects for a normal (wider) social life; thus, the majority of an officer's social life is confined to his or her own professional circle.

Policing can be an isolating profession. As Malcolm Sparrow notes, the long hours and rotating shifts push officers into each other's company, reinforcing a closed, defensive organizational culture. It is important that advocates also understand these dynamics when attempting to influence change.

Promoting change in policing requires an appreciation of the many demands on officers, from community members and other advocacy organizations, to their sergeants and the district attorney. At the same time that advocates present their case for improved response to domestic violence, other interests from crimes against the elderly and drunk driving, to speeding on Main Street, computer fraud, and Internet crimeswill vie for police attention.

Advocates attempting to influence police practice must acknowledge that they know little about what police work is truly like. Like most of the public, our understanding of police work is derived largely from fiction: television, movies, and best-selling novels. While there is a thread of truth in the images of nonstop, sensational calls, it is a limited and one-dimensional view. Policing is far more complex in the nature and breadth of its interactions with the public. Like any profession, police officers resist uninformed outsiders telling them what to do. Advocates in a battered women's shelter would be taken aback, and more than a little defensive, if the local police department appeared with a list of policy and training demands dictating how the shelter should be run. Our negotiations and discussions about police reform will lack credibility, if not accuracy, if we cannot show some familiarity with the realities of the job. To develop a better understanding of policing, advocates should seize opportunities to ride with patrol officers and observe officers in other assignments.

Most officers, however, acknowledge a level of public accountability for police that is higher than for other governmental agencies. They accept that it is reasonable to hold police work to a higher standard because of their authority to detain and use force.

Increasingly, as community-policing strategies are adopted, some police organizations are redefining their roles to reflect stronger expectations of community service. This, in turn, attracts police recruits who have different backgrounds and expectations than their predecessors. In the end, the most effective way to change police attitudes may be through recruitment and selection. Advocates should work to ensure that police departments recruit officers who bring or can develop a high-level awareness of the dynamics of violence against women. Ideally, new officers will come from diverse backgrounds and life experiences, and will possess the curiosity to welcome new approaches and ideas.

## Function

Organizational change comes from altering how people see their function in the criminal justice system and how they carry out the work assigned to them. Advocates who want to alter the way criminal justice institutions respond to domestic violence need to understand the role of each practitioner, the connections between them, and the significance of structure, policy, and training.

For example, if dispatchers see their function as managing trafficdirecting individual officers to respond to isolated calls for servicethey will not gather the information needed to successfully prosecute a crime, or to protect officers and the public. However, if dispatchers see their function as the start of an investigative process, they will ask questions that initiate evidence collection and enhance officer and victim safety. Their tapes and logs can provide evidence that corroborates injuries, documents a caller's fear for her safety, and identifies possible witnesses. Dispatchers who operate in the broader context of an investigation will inform responding officers about possible weapons, prior calls, and any restraining orders on record.

They will be the first link in establishing probable cause for arrest.

If police officers see their function as getting in and out of a domestic violence call quickly without having to come back during their shift, they will not be concerned with establishing probable cause for an arrest or collecting evidence to support prosecution. If their role is to diffuse the immediate situation and get on to the next call, there is little time to provide victim support. They may actually discourage a victim's involvement by questioning whether she wants to "press charges," pointing out how inconvenient it will be, or leaving the impression that they might arrest her if they have to return. They may resort to dual arrest instead of investigating questions of self-defense or predominant aggressor.

## Job Structure

The mechanics of a job must also be included in reform efforts. It is essential, albeit sometimes difficult, to alter the patterns by which practitioners collect and share information. Forms, procedures, and regulations are the backbones of institutions, and largely shape practitioners' priorities. Any discipline, including law enforcement, has a rigid system of information collection and documentation. What a report or form asks for, and who sees it, greatly influences what questions are asked and documentedor never asked at all.

Existing police structures tend to be mechanistic and highly centralized. Headquarters is the brain that does the thinking for the whole organization.

In the short term, this structure might promote top-down changes in policy that direct officers to respond to domestic violence calls in a prescribed way. There are some long-term problems with this process, however, as Sparrow notes.

New ideas are never conceived, evaluated, and implemented in the same place, so they are seldom "owned" or pursued enthusiastically by those in contact with the community. This approach allows for no sensitivity either on a district level (i.e., to the special needs of the community) or on an individual level (i.e., to the particular considerations of one case).

## Professional Literature

Literature, discussion, and research in the field influence every profession. Knowing where police get their information is an important element in the change process. On a local level, it means understanding and contributing to the sources of information that shape policy and practice. On a national level, it means questioning research which misses the nature of domestic violence and its significance to police response.

For most patrol officers, professional literature is not the academic publications such as the *American Journal of Police* or *Journal of Family Violence*. The everyday sources of information are trade journals, such as *Police Chief, Police, Law and Order, Law Enforcement News, Crime Control Digest, Community Policing Exchange,* and the *FBI Law Enforcement Bulletin*. Practitioners, those whose daily and primary job is policing, usually contribute to these publications. The articles are not research studies, but reports on different opinions, tactics, or policies the author holds or has experienced.

Trade journal articles focus increasingly on a proactive police response, accepting as a given that police will respond to domestic violence as a crime. The question they pose is not whether to become involved, but how to do so most effectively. They are a good source of information for advocates seeking to learn more about police response and develop training resources. While police officers are also influenced by academic journals, most professionals in the criminal justice system are exposed to research studies by means of popular reports. If the media account is weak, uncritical, or promotes a single or simplified aspect of the research, few officers, like most of us, will go beyond it to examine the source. They are also unlikely, lacking both time and access, to seek out analyses and critiques from sources who can review research within the context of working with women who have been battered.

The Internet offers police and advocates access to an ever-growing body of literature about policing and domestic violence.

The National Criminal Justice Reference Center, for example, provides on-line access and printable versions of National Institute of Justice research findings and publications by the Office of Community Oriented Policing, Office of Justice Programs, and other federal agencies, plus links to many related sites.

## WORKING WITH POLICE: GENERAL GUIDELINES

In addition to understanding the elements of change discussed in the Introductionattitudes, function, structure, and literaturesome specific techniques will help you develop a relationship with the police in your community and further your efforts to make real change. These guidelines have a *tried-and-true* quality, having been articulated almost twenty years ago by Nancy Loving and used by many advocates in the intervening decades. They apply equally to working with other parts of the criminal justice system: prosecutors, courts, and corrections. Loving's advice meshes well with the qualities of community policing: partnership, collaboration, and problem solving.

- Develop a factual understanding of the nature and scope of domestic violence in your community: number of calls to law enforcement, number of women seeking shelter and other services, examples of the violence and abuse women experience, response of other criminal justice agencies, and services available to victims and offenders.
- Document agency practices, such as: how many calls come in, how they are classified, how many arrests are made, who is arrested, the kinds of referrals made, when reports are written, and the kind of investigation conducted in domestic violence cases.
- Identify problem areas: are police not responding, not investigating, not arresting, and not making reports? Are police arresting victims? If there are problems with policy compliance with policies, how widespread is the problem?

Is it a matter of certain shifts, officers, or types of calls? Is it a misunderstanding about policy or law?

- Give careful thought to how problems are identified. Sharing stories around the lunch table is one way, but it's not the most complete source of information. A single case or incident may or may not reflect system-wide problems. Requests to change policy or practice must be grounded in sound problem identification, using a variety of data collection methods, depending upon the scope and breadth of the issue. These might include surveys of support groups, focus group discussions, ride-alongs and interviews with officers, or analysis of multiple police reports.
- Research the players: know the individuals and agencies, the control they exercise, and their decision-making authority.
- Select a type of approach based upon the community and the law enforcement agencies and individuals: collaborate, campaign, or confront, or do all three, in response to the issues and police response. Give careful thought to specific strategies.
- Identify potential supporters both within the law enforcement agency and throughout the community.
- Prioritize your change efforts. Be realistic, yet challenging, and be clear about what's most important.
- Think ahead: know what you want to come out of every meeting and what action you will take if your proposals are rejected or your strategy fails.

Not every situation or interaction with police requires that you use all these techniques. In a community where little has been done to establish a coordinated response to domestic violence, or where police have been resistant to changing their practices, advocates may have to try a series of strategies before finding the most effective. In a community where police participation has been proactive and thorough, it may be enough to identify problem areas and bring them to the attention of police managers.

## COMMUNITY POLICING AND ADVOCATE-POLICE PARTNERSHIPS

Since the mid-1980s, the United States has seen significant exploration of the function and structure of police work. Anyone attempting to influence agency policy and action should understand the principles of and recent discussions about community policing.

Community policing emphasizes a police agency's partnership with the community it serves. Police priorities are set by means of consultations with the public. Under community policing, the scope of police actions broadens: no longer are officers focused solely on their immediate responses to isolated calls for service, but are assuming wider problem-solving and prevention responsibilities.

Community policing alters the mechanics of police work by valuing the local or neighborhood beat officer and an array of skills not traditionally associated with patrol work: interviewing and interpersonal communication, mobilizing and building self-respect among communities, and analytical and problem-solving skills.

Problem-solving policing emphasizes "the power of thoughtfulness and analysis when applied across the whole spectrum of police activity." It changes the basic unit of police work from the isolated incident to the interconnected problem. It alters the structure of police work by emphasizing creativity, analysis, and evaluationa redefined role for patrol officers.

While not every police agency has adopted a community problem-solving approach to its work, these ideas are becoming increasingly widespread, influencing police structure and service delivery in many ways. Advocates must be aware of these trends in order to understand the agencies in their communities, to influence change, and to make the best case possible for greater police involvement in the community response to domestic violence.

With the 1994 Crime Bill, the Clinton Administration promised to put "100,000 new cops on the beat," with an orientation toward community partnerships and problem-solving, and an emphasis on prevention. The Department of Justice established the COPS Office (Community Oriented Policing Services) to administer hiring grants and related programs.

The impact of this activity on police job structure and response has been mixed. As noted in the Urban Institute's evaluation of the first four years of the COPS program, "adoption of community policing has very different meanings in different jurisdictions." Another commentator, David Carter, has noted that police leaders and their agencies have different motivations in claiming the community-policing label. Some have sincerely embraced it as the best means of maintaining community safety. They have committed resources beyond COPS funding, taken risks to explore new ways of doing things, and made organizational changes to support it. According to Carter, however, this commitment is not the norm.

Other agencies have experimented with community policing without any full commitment or immersion in the ideas. They are driven by small groups of enthusiastic individuals, but suffer from organizational conflict and inconsistency about what it means. Yet another, perhaps smaller, group of agencies has adopted community policing in name, but not in spirit, to obtain federal money. Advocates should discern what motivates the police agency in their community, since that may influence the genuineness of their partnership.

Along with the hiring grants, COPS funded a range of special projects, including over 300 domestic violence grants to support local partnerships among police, victim advocates, and other community organizations. This spending and attention has not necessarily improved police understanding of domestic violence among all of its recipients, however. Community policing, like "traditional" policing, can deny or ignore the context of battered women's lives, the complexity of problems they face, and the many strategies required to achieve safety.

Community policing usually results in an increased willingness on the part of police to explore partnerships and incorporate the expertise of battered womens advocates into their response to domestic violence. Communities with stronger collaborations and improved police responsesuch as Chicago, Colorado Springs, Knoxville, San Diego, Duluth, San Francisco, Madison, Portland, and Seattle have embraced community policing, at least to the level of experimentation, if not full commitment. In a growing number of communities, the response to domestic violence has become more proactive and reflective of community engagement, problem solving, and prevention. Partnerships and collaboration have also been reinforced and required under Violence Against Women Act grants.

These partnerships have varying degrees of depth, however. Some have been more grant-driven than organic. The Urban Institute's findings about police-community partnerships can also apply to those between police and advocates: "all too often, partnerships were in name only or simply standard, temporary working arrangements." The Colorado Springs Domestic Violence Enhanced Response Team is distinctive in that its police leadership acknowledges the difficulty in building equal partnerships. According to Detective Howard Black, "the hardest part of my job is trying to [create an environment] where the advocate has the same power as the cop or the prosecutor."

## ARREST AND COMMUNITY INTERVENTION

Since the release of the Minneapolis arrest study in 1984, arrest has dominated the discussion about police response to domestic violence. Twenty-three states and the District of Columbia now mandate arrest in certain misdemeanor domestic violencetiases. In eight states, preferred arrest is the law. Thirty-one states mandate arrest for order of protection violations. Arrest has become one of the key responses to domestic violence. Therefore, advocates seeking to change policy and practice should be familiar with relevant research and analysis.

The replication studies that followed the Minneapolis experiment are popularly considered to devalue arrest in domestic violence crimes. Like the issue itself, however, the findings are far more complicated and must be examined in the context of the dynamics of domestic violence and the principles of coordinated community intervention.

Well before the Minneapolis study, battered women's advocates urged police to treat domestic violence as criminal conduct and to arrest assailants when they had probable cause to do so. They wanted police to apply their professional knowledge and skills to domestic violence cases, just as they did to other types of calls. They wanted police to know the criminal laws available to them and to use their interviewing, evidence collection, and report writing skills. The experiences of battered women and the inaction of police led many advocates to prefer systematic arrest, for many reasons.

- Immediate arrest can prevent further or more serious injury.
- Arrest can result in less repeat violence.
- Arrest promotes a consistent police response and helps eliminate officer bias based upon the offender's position in the community.
- Arrest can lead to more prosecution and support increased convictions and guilty pleas.
- Arrest focuses police and community attention on domestic violence as serious criminal behavior.
- When applied consistently and without bias, arrest extends equal protection under the law to battered women.
- Arrest increases a woman's safety by challenging her partner's belief that it is acceptable to assault her.
- Arrest can break through a woman's isolation and give her the message that there is support and protection for her in the community.
- Arrest reinforces legal sanctions against violence.
- Arrest is part of the larger effort to change the cultural acceptance of violence in intimate relationships.

At the same time, advocates were very aware of the liabilities and problems with mandatory arrest-namely, relying on a system whose traditional response has been inaction and victim blaming:

- Arrest gives police more authority over community members and can be used unfairly against battered women, people of color, and the poor.
- Arrest does not necessarily keep assailants away from their victims.
- Arrest does not guarantee that domestic violence crimes will be prosecuted properly.
- Arrest may discourage women from calling the police because they do not want their partners arrested.
- Arrest may discourage lesbians and gay men from calling the police because of the subsequent public record and possible prosecution.
- Arrest does not guarantee that officers will prepare good reports or be prepared to testify.
- Danger to women may increase if arrest occurs in the absence of shelters or safe homes.
- Arrest may spark police backlash with victims arrested under "mutual combat" claims.

Advocates have long known that arrest, standing alone, may not make a difference. Arrest has been most effective when it has been implemented as part of a comprehensive approach that also includes individual support and advocacy for women; systematic prosecution, sentencing, and monitoring of abusers; a specialized court-ordered abuser counseling program; interagency coordination, policy development, and monitoring; and, law enforcement training, reporting, and monitoring of domestic violence calls. Arrest is only one part of the community change process necessary to challenge domestic violence. It cannot be the single focus.

Anyone attempting to change police practice must understand the complexities of arrest and how it might influence women's safety. Managing mandatory arrest laws or policies means asking victims what happened: Did arrest make a difference? Why? Why not? It means respecting their observations and the implications for policy change, further police training, and improved victim services.

The quality of officer-public interaction is one example of this complexity that the arrest studies overlooked. They isolated police response into narrow acts of arrest, separation, and mediation, disconnected from police attitudes toward and interactions with the parties involved, as well as the larger history of police-community relations.

How do officers treat people? What effect does the officer have on the victim and suspect? Does it make a difference if an officer is disinterested or hostile? The arrest studies did not address these questions. One critique noted that "the studies may in some ways distort rather than clarify our understanding of different police responses to domestic violence," and noted three ways in which this happens:

1. By isolating one factor - arrest - from the larger context of domestic violence and the criminal justice system's response.
2. By reducing the subjects of the study to statistics and thus losing the important information which could be provided by the voices of the victims themselves.
3. By analyzing both the problem under study and the potential police implications solely in individualist, non-relational terms.

If they are to be accountable to battered women, arrest laws and policies must have the following oversight: close and consistent monitoring; training on the policy throughout the agency-from dispatchers to supervisors to patrol officers; training on problem areas such as dual arrest and the concepts of self-defense and primary physical aggressor; and exchange of information and experiences with other communities. Police practice, including arrest, will maximize safety only when it occurs within th econtext of community intervention developed around these key components:

1. A coherent philosophical approach centralizing victim safety

2. "Best practice" policies and protocols for intervention agencies that are part of an integrated response
3. Enhanced networking among service providers
4. Monitoring and tracking built into the system
5. A supportive community infrastructure for battered women
6. Sanctions and rehabilitation opportunities for abusers
7. Strategies to undo the harm violence to women does to children
8. Evaluation of the coordinated community response from the standpoint of victim safety

The Duluth Domestic Abuse Intervention Project developed the Safety and Accountability Audit to address the need for oversight of police and criminal justice system intervention. A Safety Audit is a systematic investigation of institutional response to domestic violence. Conducted by multi-disciplinary teams, it involves several methods: mapping the response to domestic violence cases and the different systems' roles, actions, and relationships; observation of that response, such as police ride-along, 911 processing, and booking; interviews with practitioners in various systems; focus group discussions with battered women, practitioners, and community members; and text analysis of the "paper trails"-the information collected, shared, and used by people within the same or related systems, such as 911 and dispatch transcripts, police reports, and pre-sentence reports.

An audit can be limited to single step, such as the method by which a victim is notified of an offender's release from jail, or it can examine a series of steps. For example, a Safety Audit could be conducted on dual arrest cases, including all steps from the 911 call to the police report to the prosecutor's action. Alternately, it could help determine what happens when a suspect is gone when police arrive. It can also be used to examine broad issues, such as a system's response to specific groups of people. It could be used, for example, to investigate the experience of communities of color or the system's response to children in domestic violence cases. The information collected is analyzed to determine whether and how to change or develop policies, administrative procedures, laws, system linkages, training, technology, and underlying assumptions.

## POLICY AND TRAINING MODELS

Policy is a statement of how police are expected to conduct their business. A policy on any given subject might be a paragraph or two, or it might run to twenty pages, depending upon an organization's approach, the subject covered, and the level of detail needed to outline implementation. The operational needs and philosophy of the agency determine some policies, such as when officers can or must carry weapons off-duty. State legislatures dictate other policies. In Wisconsin, for example, police departments must have written policies on the use of force, vehicle pursuits, complaints, and domestic violence. Eighteen states now require local written policies for handling domestic violence cases.

*The International Association of Chiefs of Police (IACP), as part of its National Law Enforcement Policy Center, has issued model policies covering domestic violence and domestic violence by police officers. Released in 1990 and revised in 1996, the IACP package includes a model policy, Domestic Violence Concepts and Issues Paper, and a training key. It was designed to provide direction and training resources for agencies working on a domestic violence policy. In 1999, the IACP released a similar model and background paper on officer involved domestic violence.*

No single model fits every agency or locale. The IACP provides a blueprint from which police or sheriff's departments can build or revise their own policies, adapted to fit their communities. It provides guidelines and direction, but must be tailored to each community. It sets standards and recommendations for police response with which advocates should be familiar.

*The Internet provides access to several law enforcement domestic violence policies and related information, including:* New York State Model Domestic Violence Policy: Guidelines for Criminal Justice, Legal, and Judicial Systems, *the Metropolitan Nashville*

Police Department policy, Model Policy for Kentucky Law Enforcement, the San Diego Police Department's domestic violence manual, and model policies for Wisconsin agencies, which operate under a mandatory arrest law with a primary physical aggressor standard. Advocates can also find the Model Code on Domestic and Family Violence from the National Council of Juvenile and Family Court Judges. This is a useful tool for assessing local policies and state law.

Domestic Violence Protocol for Law Enforcement adopted by the Santa Clara (CA) County Police Chief's Association is an example of a comprehensive policy, and one that is available in several formats on the Internet. It is distinctive in that it has been developed across jurisdictional lines, with the goal of achieving consistency in agency response across the county. The protocol is a comprehensive document that includes definitions, common charges, and detailed expectations for dispatch and patrol officer response, as well as follow-up investigations, restraining orders, and victim assistance. It also addresses situations in which the suspect is a law enforcement officer, a juvenile, or in the military.

It has become the standard in police agencies to define domestic violence as a crime and to require arrest under probable cause. Policies developed in the past ten years, therefore, tend to be variations on mandatory arrest, requiring that officers shall, must, will or should arrest. Whether or not a policy is written with a mandatory or preferred arrest point of view will depend upon state law, departmental philosophy, and community participation. Battered women's advocates have an opportunity to influence policy by becoming well versed in a variety of models and approaches.

## TRAINING

While policy states expectations, training is crucial to developing the knowledge and skills necessary to make policy a reality. Training is also a mechanism for addressing compliance problems after implementation.

Training police officers to implement a domestic violence policy or improve their practices cannot be left to advocates alone, nor should it be conducted by police officers alone. A multi-disciplinary team approach not only models partnership and collaboration, but also is more likely to engage the audience. Ideally, the domestic violence training team includes a police officer who can speak to the concerns of responding officers, a prosecutor to cover legal aspects, and a community advocate who can speak to why battered women might act as they do once police get involved.

Information about the characteristics of domestic violence can be interspersed with discussions about initial response, investigation, report writing, officer safety, and arrest procedures. To reinforce the training goals and avoid contradictions, all team members should understand the dynamics of domestic violence, the role and experiences of patrol officers and other participants, and their jurisdiction's legal authority to intervene. Real-life scenarios allow officers to develop a common understanding of what the policy means, how to implement it, and who to consult with questions.

It is critical that police training be conducted within the context of police work. Advocates can count on having an audience that will be blunt and eager for useful information. This is not the time for an extended lecture on the theoretical framework of battering. It will not be well received by participants and is likely to create a barrier that cannot be overcome by the training that follows. It is also critical that instructors be prepared, knowledgeable, and well versed in adult learning and facilitation.

The train-the-trainer curriculum developed by the Federal Law Enforcement Training Center, Domestic Violence: A Rural Law Enforcement Response, begins with an orientation to adult learning and appropriate activities and facilitation techniques. The arrest curriculum available from the California Alliance Against Domestic Violence also includes material on facilitation strategies and overcoming common training problems. The video exercises developed for the course conclude with advice from veteran trainers, almost all of whom at one point describe the stereotypical police audience: everyone clustered at the back of the room, arms crossed or reading the paper. They emphasize the importance of participation versus talking at the audience: "let them teach themselves and each other." Their advice includes:

- Know your audience and appreciate that there will be diverse opinions.
- Stay flexible.
- Assess their needs: What are their issues and questions?
- Set a positive tone and be sincere.
- Address concerns up front.
- Take control of the classroom environment.
- Do not take it personally if someone challenges you, but use it to teach.
- Avoid the biggest mistake: failure to prepare.

As one instructor noted, if you do not know the subject and are not prepared, you should not be teaching. "The best curriculum in the world means nothing if the trainer is no good."

Domestic Violence: The Law Enforcement Response was developed by the Duluth Domestic Abuse Intervention Project in 1988 and has been used widely throughout the Untied States. Revised in 1998, it is an example of a comprehensive training format, built on adult learning principles. It includes an instructor's manual and preparation video, student guide, and videotaped scenarios of officers responding to a variety of domestic violence calls. Targeted to patrol officers, it covers the dynamics of domestic violence and the range of police intervention procedures: interviews, determining primary aggression, evidence collection (including strangulation, harassment, and stalking), and report writing.

Many training resources have emerged over the past twenty years as communities have developed domestic violence intervention projects and the Violence Against Women Act and the COPS Office have provided grants. Videos, curricula, and manuals provide training on policy development, victim safety, offender accountability, investigation, and coordinated community response. They address specific problems that have emerged as arrest policies have been implemented, such as inappropriate dual arrests and misunderstanding the concept of primary physical aggressor.

Most state domestic violence coalitions can cite communities in their state that model sound police training. No single curriculum will fit all circumstances, so advocates should be familiar with several models. Introducing a new policy or change in the law may be accomplished best in one format while addressing problems with evidence collection or dual arrests may require a different approach. Training 911 and dispatch operators will be different from training sergeants and other supervisors.

Any curriculum must be adapted to the needs of the community, the training issues, and state law. By searching out a variety of models that are well grounded in the principles of victim safety, offender accountability, and community change, advocates can more effectively collaborate with police to develop training that facilitates changes in policy and practice, as well as addresses specific problems that emerge with changing police response, such as dual arrests or incomplete reports.

## CONCLUSION

Battered women's advocates have repeatedly challenged the police to make significant changes in their response to domestic violence. Where they have succeeded, advocates have acted with an understanding of the structure and function of police work, appreciation for the demands on police time and attention, and solid, documented analyses of problems and recommendations for change.

In many communities today, the level of agency dialogue and collaboration, and the extent to which they support battered women, could barely be imagined twenty years ago. Advocates in other communities, however, continue to face entrenched resistance and rampant victim blaming. Throughout the country, advocates are confronted with the daily challenge of putting the needs of battered women first, ahead of criminal justice system demands to process arrests, cases, and convictions.

We have learned that police can be agents of change. They can reshape institutional policies and practices. They can be allies to advocates in improving safety for battered women. Where this has happened, advocates and police have worked through disagreement and conflict, but they have stayed at the table, willing to continue the discussion and take risks in building relationships with one another. As one advocate observed, "there is no magic potion to pour down people's throats; it's hard work over a long haul and sometimes success is measured by everyone being willing to sit in the same room together."

# Bibliography


Afkhami, Mahnaz and Haleh Vaziri. (1996) *Claiming Our Rights: A Manual for Women's Human Rights Education in Muslim Societies*, Bethesda, Maryland, USA: Sisterhood is Global Institute.

Amnesty International. (2000) *Respect, Protect, Fulfill Women's Human Rights: State responsibility for abuses by 'non-state actors,'* London, United Kingdom: Amnesty International.

Ashworth, Georgina. (1993) *Changing the Discourse: A Guide to Women and Human Rights*, London, UK: CHANGE.

Benninger-Budel, Carin (2000) *Violence against Women: 10 Reports/Year 2000 For the Protection and Promotion of the Human Rights of Women*, Geneva, Switzerland: World Organisation Against Torture.

*Beyond Victims and Villains: Addressing Sexual Violence in the Education Sector*, Panos Institute, 2003.

Brasileiro, Ana Maria. (1997) *Women Against Violence: Breaking the Silence*, New York, NY, USA: United Nations Development Fund for Women (UNIFEM).

Center for the Study of Human Rights. (1996) *Women and Human Rights: The Basic Documents*, New York, NY, USA: Center for the Study of Human Rights.

Center for Women's Global Leadership. (1994) *Gender Violence and Women's Human Rights in Africa: A Symposium*, New Brunswick, NJ, USA: Center for Women's Global Leadership.

Clarke, Roberta. (1998) *Violence Against Women in the Caribbean: State and Non-State Responses*, New York, NY, USA:

United Nations Development Fund for Women (UNIFEM).

Cook, Rebecca J. ed. (1994) *Human Rights of Women: National and International Perspectives,* Philadelphia, PA, USA: University of Pennsylvania Press.

Corrin, Chris ed. (1996) *Women in a Violent World: Feminist Analysis and Resistance Across 'Europe,'* Edinburgh, Scotland: Edinburgh University Press.

Davies, Miranda ed. (1994) *Women and Violence: Realities and Responses Worldwide,* London/Atlantic Highlands: Zed Books Ltd. Contact: Women, Ink. or Zed Books Ltd.,

Elson, Diane ed. (2000) *Progress of the World's Women 2000,* New York, NY, USA: United Nations Development Fund for Women (UNIFEM).

Family Violence Prevention Fund and Center for Women's Global Leadership. (1997) *Migrant Women's Human Rights in G-7 Countries: Organizing Strategies,* New Brunswick, NJ, USA: Center for Women's Global Leadership.

Finney Hayward, Ruth (2000) *Breaking the Earthenware Jar: Lessons from South Asia to End Violence against Women and Girls,* New York, NY USA: United Children's Fund (UNICEF).

Fisher, Elizabeth and Linda Gray MacKay. (1996) *Gender Justice: Women's Rights are Human Rights,* Cambridge, MA, USA: Unitarian Universalist Service Committee.

Green, December. (1999) *Gender Violence in Africa: African Women's Responses,* New York, NY, USA: St. Martin's Press.

International Gay and Lesbian Human Rights Commission. (1995) *Unspoken Rules: Sexual Orientation and Women's Human Rights,* San Francisco, California, USA: International Gay and Lesbian Human Rights Commission (IGLHRC).

Kempadoo, Kamala and Jo Doezema eds. (1998) *Global Sex Workers: Rights, Resistance and Redefinition,* New York, NY, USA: Routledge.

Latin American and Caribbean Women's Health Network. (1996) *The Right to Live Without Violence: Women's Proposals and Actions, Women's Health Collection,* Vol 1: Latin American and

Caribbean Women's Health Network.

Ikkaracan, Pinar ed. (2000) *Women and Sexuality in Muslim Societies*, Istanbul, Turkey: Women for Women's Human Rights (WWHR).

Maramba, Petronella, Bisi Olateru-Olagbegi and Rosalie Tiani Webanenou. (1995) *Structural Adjustment Programs and the Human Rights of African Women*, Harare, Zimbabwe: Women in Law and Development in Africa (WiLDAF).

Naraghi Anderlini, Sanam. (2000) *Women at the Peace Table: Making a Difference*, New York, NY, USA: United Nations Development Fund for Women (UNIFEM).

Petchesky, Rosalind and Karen Judd eds. (1998) *Negotiating Reproductive Rights: Women's Perspectives across Countries and Cultures*, New York, NY: International Reproductive Rights Research and Action Group.

Rehn, Elisabeth and Ellen Johnson Sirleaf. (2002) *Progress of the World's Women 2002: Women War Peace, The Independent Experts' Assessment on the Impact of Armed Conflict on Women and Women's Role in Peace-Building*, New York, NY, USA: United Nations Development Fund for Women.

Reilly, Niamh. (1996) *Without Reservation: The Beijing Tribunal on Accountability for Women's Human Rights*, New Brunswick, NJ, USA: Center for Women's Global Leadership.

Rothschild, Cynthia (2000) *Written Out: How Sexuality is Used to Attack Women's Organizing*, New York, NY, USA: International Gay and Lesbian Human Rights Commission (IGLHRC) and Center for Women's Global Leadership.

Sajor, Indai Lourdes ed. (1998) *Common Grounds: Violence Against Women in War and Armed Conflict Situations*, Philippines: Asian Centre for Women's Human Rights (ASCENT).

Schuler, Margaret ed. (1992) *Freedom from Violence: Women's Strategies from Around the World*, New York, NY, USA: United Nations Development Fund for Women (UNIFEM).

Sweetman, Caroline, ed. (1998) *Violence Against Women*, Oxford, United Kingdom: OXFAM International.

Thomas, Dorothy Q. (1996) *All Too Familiar: Sexual Abuse of Women in U.S. State Prisons,* New York, NY, USA: Human Rights Watch (HRW).

Tomasevski, Katarina. (1993) *Women and Human Rights,* London/Atlantic Highlands: Zed Books Ltd.

Turshen, Meredith and Clotilde Twagiramariya, eds. (1998) *What Women Do in Wartime: Gender and Conflict in Africa,* London/Atlantic Highlands: Zed Books.

United Nations Development Fund for Women (UNIFEM). (1999) *Women@Work to End Violence: Voices in Cyberspace,* New York, NY, USA: UNIFEM.

United Nations Development Fund for Women (UNIFEM). (2003) *Not a Minute More: Ending Violence Against Women,* New York, NY, USA: UNIFEM.

United Nations High Commissioner for Refugees. (1995) *Sexual Violence Against Refugees: Guidelines on Prevention and Response,* Geneva, Switzerland: High Commissioner for Refugees.

United Nations. (1996) Platform for Action and the Beijing Declaration, New York, NY, USA: Department of Public Information.

Watts, Charlotte, Susanna Osam and Everjoice Win, eds. (1995) *The Private is Public: A Study of Violence Against Women in Southern Africa,* Harare, Zimbabwe: Women in Law and Development in Africa (WiLDAF).

Wolper, Andrea and Julie S. Peters. (1995) *Women's Rights, Human Rights: International Feminist Perspectives,* New York, NY, USA: Routledge.

# Index

**A**

Adverse Pregnancy Outcomes, 26.
Agency Response Checklists, 70.
Alcohol and Drug Use, 35, 138.

**B**

Barriers to Addressing, Violence, 41.
Basic Models of Specialization, 83.

**C**

Changing Community Norms, 63.
Changing Policies, 149.
Child Custody, 172, 176, 180, 192.
Civil Orders of Protection, 167.
Communication Campaigns, 52.
Community Health Promotion, 51.
Community Intervention, 184, 205.
Community Policing, 193, 194, 195.
Condom Negotiation, 25.
Contraceptive Use, 22.
Costs to Abusers, 56.
Costs to the Economy, 37.
Courts, 44, 62, 68, 69, 70, 83, 84, 85, 87, 89, 91, 92, 94, 106, 110, 114, 115, 117, 165, 167, 170, 178, 179, 180, 181, 185, 191.
Criminal Domestic Violence Courts, 83.
Criminal Protection Orders, 163.
Cultural Stereotypes, 42.

**D**

Death Review Team Protocols, 145.
Depression, 16, 31, 33, 34, 35, 129, 133.
Dispatcher Response, 72.
Domestic Violence, 35, 39, 53, 63, 65, 83, 84, 85, 86, 87,

88, 91, 93, 100, 105, 106, 116, 121, 123, 127, 131, 133, 134, 135, 136, 140, 141, 143, 144, 160, 176, 195, 200, 201, 202, 203.
Dynamics of Abuse, 5.

**E**

Enforceable Order, 157, 159.
Enforcing Court, 157.
Enforcing Jurisdiction, 158, 159, 163, 165, 169, 171, 173, 174, 175, 179, 181.
Enforcing Protection Orders, 158.

**F**

Fatality Review Team, 122, 133, 140, 143.
Federal Law, 165, 167, 169, 170, 171, 173, 174, 178, 180.
Firearms Considerations, 159.
Forced Sex in Marriage, 13.
Full Faith and Credit, 157, 160, 161, 162, 163, 164, 165, 166, 167, 168, 169, 170, 174.

**G**

Gender-based Abuse, 37.

**H**

Health Providers, 40.
High-Risk Pregnancies, 28.
High-Risk Sexual Behavior, 22.

**I**

Initial Officer Response, 73.
Institutional Constraints, 42.
Intent of the Law, 162.
Interstate Stalking, 177.
Interstate Travel, 176.
Intimate Partner Abuse, 3, 9.

**J**

Job Structure, 189.
Justice System Response, 65.

**L**

Law Enforcement Response, 71, 202, 203.

**M**

Monitoring Change, 149.
Mutual Orders, 158, 167.

**N**

Negative Social Attitudes, 42, 43.

**O**

Order of Protection, 137, 154, 164, 167, 168, 170, 171, 173, 178, 179, 180, 195.

**P**

Perinatal Transmission, 27.

Post-traumatic Stress Disorder, 34.
Probation, 84, 86, 89, 93, 100, 101, 102, 103, 104, 105, 106, 107, 112, 116, 119, 123, 124, 163, 169.
Protection Across Jurisdictions, 161.

**S**

Sacramento Home Court, 96, 97.
Safety Planning, 68, 78, 153, 166.
Sexual Abuse in Childhood, 15, 24.
Sexual abuse in childhood, 24.
Sexual Autonomy, 19.
Sexual Coercion, 3, 12, 19, 54.
Signs of Abuse, 51.
Strategic Screening, 48.
Suicide, 16, 26, 29, 33, 34, 121, 122, 123, 125, 126, 130, 131, 133, 134, 140, 152, 166.

**T**

Tribal Orders, 158.

**U**

Unwanted Pregnancies, 19.

**V**

Victim-Centered Approach, 79.
Voluntary Counseling, 26.

